LAKSHIT

Jainism

Anwsers For The Questions!

Contents

Preface

In the sixth century, BC Buddhism had just been founded. The Vedic religion was almost getting extinct and Hinduism, as we know it today, was at a nebulous stage. Jainism at that time was not only a mature and living religion but also one claiming hoary antiquity. All its tenets had fully developed by that time and these tenets have remained almost unchanged all these 2500 years. Jainism is thus the oldest living religion of India.

But age alone is not what gives importance to Jainism. This religion is important because it has greatly influenced practically all-religious thinking of India. If, as is thought by many, the spirit of Indian religious life was 'life and world negating' it might be said that it was mainly due to the influence of Jainism and similar other religions of that time on Indian thought. It also shows the triumph of the *Jain* spirit over the 'life and world-affirming' attitude of the Vedic people who failed to divert the mainstream of Indian religious thinking from pessimism to an optimistic and joyous path. The aversion to the killing of animals, the belief that all ascetics are holy people (and conversely that a person in order to be holy should be an ascetic), the theory of the transmigration of the soul, and that 'getting born in this world is itself a punishment' all these are parts of Hindu thinking. They seem to have been adopted without much change from Jainism and similar other religions that existed in India in the sixth century BC. (The evidence of the existence of such religions, though scanty, is available from the Buddhist and *Jain* texts.

Yet, the *Jain*s constitute a small proportion of the Indian people. They probably number a little over three million in a population of nearly 700 million. How did such a small community exercise so much influence? The answer probably lies in the fact that the original religions of the Indian people at least from the Indus Valley times were similar in many respects to Jainism. These religions got somewhat modified by the impact of the Vedic cult, but ultimately the ancient religions of India, of which Jainism was one, prevailed Jainism has thus not so much influenced as provided a guide-post to Hinduism to get back to its original course.

Since Jainism itself has not much changed or

developed in the course of these 2,500 years, it has in a sense no history. The last change in Jainism was introduced by Mahavira himself when he proposed an additional vow to the original four vows of Parshva the immediately- preceding *Tirthankara*. The *Jain*s themselves recognized this absence of change by hesitating to write any history of their religion after Mahavira. Indeed, when the *Digambaras* write any history (or mythology) of their religion they stop with Mahavira. The *Svetambaras* do not doubt at least two works, which continue the history even after Mahavira, but these too stop after a few centuries.

This is, therefore, a history of the *Jain* people and not so much a history of their religion.

In the history of *Jain*s, the most important figure is Mahavira. He was a contemporary of the Buddha. This we know from the Buddhist works only, for the *Jain* works never mention the Buddha. Mahavira lived for 72 years of which for the last 30 years he was a teacher. The *Jain* works give some details for the first 42 years of Mahavir's life, but tell us little about his life as a teacher. (In the case of Buddha also the Buddhist works give few details of his life after he became a teacher).

Jainism did not get much royal support in the first few centuries after Mahavira. Indeed, the Jain's themselves claim only one royal patron in these centuries. He was Samprati, grandson of Ashoka, and ruler of Ujayini. Epigraphic evidence, however, shows that Ashoka himself was a protector of the *Jain*s and had appointed officers to look after their welfare, though he may not have been a patron. Again from epigraphic evidence, we know that in the 1st century BC king Kharavela of Orissa and his queen were patrons of Jainism. (The *Jain* works mention Ashoka only in passing, and Kharavela is not known to them at all). People engaged in commerce and trades were drawn towards Jainism from at least the early centuries of the Christian era. This we know from the extensive remains of the sculptures gifted by them in the Kankalitila in Mathura.

We do not know how the *Jain*s broke into two groups, the *Digambaras,* and the *Svetambaras.* Perhaps there was no actual schism, the two groups just drifted apart due to geographical reasons, the *Jain*s of Gujarat and the neighboring areas emerging as the*Svetambaras* sometime in the 5th century AD.

By perhaps the 4th century AD Jainism had spread to South India. Southwest Karnataka from the very beginning became its center. Though the *Jain*s were found more or less all over the South, in this part of Karnataka and especially in the Tulu speaking areas, Jainism was a force to reckon with for many centuries. They received patronage from the rulers of many dynasties and occupied important administrative and military posts under them. Some of the Western *Ganga* rulers themselves became *Jain*s. There were many learned *Jain*s in the court of the kings of Karnataka. They wrote books on logic and philosophy and some of them produced important works on mathematics and medicine also.

In the matter of Architecture and Statuary, the *Jain*s produced remarkable pieces of art in several places in Karnataka and Tamil Nadu.

In the 12th century Gujarat the rulers appreciated the learning of the great *Jain* polymath Hemachandra by making him their confidant. The Gujarat *Jain*s continued the tradition of learning. In the 16th century, Abdul Fazl counted Hira Vijaya *Suri* as one of the 21 most learned persons of the Mughal Empire, and Akbar himself invited him to his court. The *Jain*s maintained their fame in visual arts. They constructed beautiful temples in Shatrunjaya, Girnar, Ranakpur, Abu, Deogarh, Khajuraho, and other places in northern India. The contribution of the *Jain*s in the cultural heritage of India has been high.

The *Jain* religious philosophy has not changed much in all these years. The only development one can think of is that they have elaborated on their logical system known as the *Syadvada*. The original enunciation of this doctrine given in the canonical literature is not very clear. The later logicians have developed it into a complete system. The important point to notice, however, is that no *Jain* author has tried to refute this doctrine or to advance a rival system. There is no controversy in Jainism comparable to the one that has been going on for centuries on the interpretation of the Hindu Vedanta-*Sutra*. It is not that there have been no differences at all among the *Jains* in the matter of their religion. There have been many groups and sub-groups within the community. But when one comes to analyze the differences among them it is found that these relate to trifling matters of ritual, or details of the mythological stories. Even the great division between the *Digambaras* and the *Svetambaras* is about such petty details.

As the *Jain* temples and monasteries grew rich with fresh endowments, the persons in charge of these establishments became powerful. New groups arose within the community to protest against such domination. One such Protestant group arose among the *Digambaras* in the Agra region in the 17th century. They were known as the *Terapanthis*. Among the *Svetambaras* also there rose a new group in the 15th century that believed that image worship was not mentioned in the canon.

These controversies have not affected the essentials of the *Jain* religion. Never the less, they have made the *Jains* think about their religion and have kept Jainism alive.

One

WHO IS GOD ?

According to Jainism, the universe was never created, nor will it ever cease to exist. It is independent and self-sufficient, does not require a creator, nor any superior power to govern it, nor a judge nor destroyer. Jainism believes in the world of gods and hell beings who are born and who die to be reborn like living beings in the earthly realm of existence.

Those souls who live in the body of a god, do so because of their positive karma. The gods live a life of happiness, fun and frolic, whose wishes are automatically fulfilled. They also possess a more transcendent knowledge about material things and can anticipate events in the human realms. However, once their past karmic merit is exhausted, the souls leave the "god body" and are reborn again as humans, animals or other beings.

Two

WHAT IS JAINISM ?

Jainism dates to the 6th century B.C.E. in India. The religion derives its name from the *jinas* ("conquerors"), a title was given to twenty-four great teachers (*Tirthankaras* or "ford-makers"), through whom their faith was revealed. Mahavira, the last of the *Tirthankaras*, is considered the founder of Jainism. The ultimate goal of Jainism the liberation of the self (*jiva*) from rebirth, which is attained through the elimination of accumulated karma (the consequences of previous actions). This occurs through both the disciplined cultivation of knowledge and control of bodily passions. When the passions have been utterly conquered and all karma has been removed, one becomes a Jina ("conqueror") and is no longer subject to rebirth.

Jainism conceives of a multi-layered universe containing both heavens and hells. Movement through these levels of the universe requires adherence to the Jainism doctrines emphasizing a peaceful and disciplined life. These principles include non-violence in all parts of life (verbal, physical, and mental), speaking truth, sexual monogamy, and detachment from material things. As part of the disciplined and non-violent lifestyle, Jains typically are strict vegetarians and often adhere to a quite arduous practice of non-violence, which restricts the sorts of occupations the may follow (no farming, for instance, since insects are inadvertently harmed in plowing). Jainism's ethical system is based on the idea that the right faith, knowledge, and conduct must be cultivated simultaneously.

Three

FIVE GREAT TEACHINGS (VOWS OF JAINISM)

To acquire the right knowledge, right faith, and right conduct, the three essential pillars of the state of liberation in Jainism, one must observe the five great teachings or vows, popularly known as the five Mahavratas:

1. Ahimsa
2. Satya
3. Acharya or Asteya
4. Brahmacharya
5. Aparigraha

Let's go into the details of these.

Ahimsa

Among the five vows, non-violence (Ahimsa) is the principle of primary importance. Ahimsa is the supreme religion in Jainism; captured very well by the expression – *Ahimsa parmo dharma*. Jain literature repeatedly observes -*"Do not injure, abuse, oppress, enslave, insult, torment, torture, or kill any creature or living being."* According to Jainism, no living being is superior or inferior to the other, regardless of its size, shape, or spiritual developments. The implication being that no living creature has the right to harm, injure, or kill any other living being, including animals, insects, and plants. This is true for any kind of violence. Even harsh words causing mental torture or thinking evil of someone is also considered violence in Jainism.

Practically, however, it is impossible to survive without killing or injuring some of the smallest living beings. Some lives are killed even when we breathe, drink water, or eat food. Therefore, when it comes to Jainism, some pieces of literature say that the minimum killing of the lowest form of life is the ideal living. Living beings, according to Jainism & as far as their order from highest to lowest living form goes, are classified based on their senses, according to Jainism.

The five senses are touch, taste, smell, sight, and

6

hearing. Based on these, the following is the order of life form from highest to lowest

1. Five senses – humans, animals, birds, heavenly and hellish beings
2. Four senses – flies, bees, etc.
3. Three senses- ants, lice, etc.
4. Two senses – worms, leaches, etc.
5. One sense – plants, water, air, earth, fire, etc.

Based on the order above, Jainism allows laypeople to use only vegetables as food for survival. Jainism preaches strict vegetarianism and prohibits non-vegetarian foods.

Satya – Truth

Jainism preaches that Untruth & Falsehood are bred when anger, greed, fear & jokes are a part of one's character. Sometimes, to speak the truth, very high courage is required. Only those who have conquered greed, fear, anger, jealousy, ego, and frivolity can speak the truth. Jainism insists that one should not only refrain from untruth, and they should feel wholesome about the truth. One should remain silent if the truth causes pain, hurt, anger, or death of any living being.

Truth should be observed at all levels by a person

vis-a-vis speech, mind, and deed. Even the promotion of an untruth is considered as bad as untruth itself.

Acharya/Asteya — Refrain from Stealing

Stealing is defined as taking someone else's property without his consent, particularly by unjust or immoral methods. One should not take anything which does not belong to them. Also taking away a thing, which may be lying, unattended or unclaimed, is considered as stealing. This vow should be observed very strictly, even for a worthless thing, which does not belong to them. Also, when accepting alms or help or aid, one should refrain from taking more than what is needed. Even taking more than one's need is considered theft in Jainism.

All in all, Asteya teaches that one should neither themselves steal nor ask others to do so, or approve any such activities.

Brahmacharya — Celibacy / Chastity

Jainism preaches one hundred % abstinence from pleasure sensual or to any of the five senses. At the time of indulgence in activities of sensual pleasure, a person sets aside all virtues and reason. This is a very difficult vow to observe; considered as the most difficult by many. A person not indulging in activities of pleasure physically, but imagining those is equally disrespectful to the teachings of Jainism.

For householders, they should not any physical relationship other than their spouse. The relationship with their spouse should be of a limited nature. For monks, strict celibacy is the only path towards spiritual liberation.

Aparigraha — Non-attachment / Non-possession

Jainism establishes that the more a person indulges in worldly wealth & possessions, the more they are likely to assert to sin to acquire this wealth. In the long run, they are most likely to be unhappy since these material possessions are futile. It is very much possible that the ones holding on to the material world are likely to succumb to greed, jealousy, selfishness, ego, hatred, violence, etc. Lord Mahavir preached that worldly material desires have no real end to them.

According to Jainism, anyone desiring spiritual liberation should withdraw themselves from all attachments to pleasing objects. These objects are classified based on which sense they are pleasing too. For true liberation, one should give away all their attachments to the following:

- Material Objects: Wealth, property, grains, house, books, clothes, etc.
- Relationships: Father, mother, spouse, children, friends, enemies, other monks, disciples, etc.
- Objects pleasing to any of the five senses: The five senses are touch, taste, smell, sight, and hearing.
- All Feelings: Pleasure and painful feelings towards any object.

One should have equanimity towards music and noise, good and bad smells, soft and hard objects for touch, beautiful and dirty sights, etc. Food should not be eaten for taste but for survival to continue to spiritual progress till attainment of liberation.

Four

THℰ SOUℒ

Jain ideas about the soul differ from those of many other religions.

The Jain word that comes closest to the soul is *jiva*, which means a conscious, living being. For Jains, body and soul are different things: the body is just an inanimate container - the conscious being is the jiva.

After each bodily death, the jiva is reborn into a different body to live another life, until it achieves liberation. When a jiva is *embodied* (i.e. in a body), it exists throughout that body and isn't found in any particular bit of it.

Jains believe:

- the soul exists forever

11

- each soul is always independent
- the soul is responsible for what it does
- the soul experiences the consequences of its actions
- the soul can become liberated from the cycle of birth and death
- not all souls can be liberated - some souls are inherently incapable of achieving this
- the soul can evolve towards that liberation by following principles of behavior

Individuality

Each jiva is an individual quite independent of other jivas. This is different from one of the Hindu Vedanta schools of belief where each soul is part of a single ultimate reality.

Jains believe that there is an infinite number of souls in the universe - every living thing, no matter how primitive, is a jiva - and at any given time many of these jivas are not embodied.

Souls have not fallen from perfection

For Jains, each jiva has been associated with matter and involved in the cycle of birth and death since the beginning of time. They did not in some way fall from perfection to become involved in this cycle.

Some jivas, through their own efforts, have become liberated and escaped from the cycle.

Liberated souls

Some jivas have achieved liberation from the cycle of samsara or reincarnation and are not reborn. They are called *Siddhas*.

Liberated jivas don't have physical bodies; they possess infinite knowledge, infinite vision, infinite power, and infinite bliss - in effect, they have become perfect beings.

This makes liberated jivas the beings most like gods in Jain belief, but they are very different from the conventional idea of gods:

- they do not create or destroy
- it's not possible to have any sort of relationship with them
- they do not intervene in the universe
- they did not set down the laws of the universe
- they do not make any demands on human beings
- they don't reward human beings in any way, or forgive their sins, or give them grace
- human beings don't owe their existence to them
- humans can only use them as an inspiration

So when Jains worship 'gods' they do so to set before themselves the example of perfection that they want to follow in their own lives.

Non-liberated souls

Every jiva has the possibility of achieving liberation, and thus of becoming a god, and each soul is involved in a process of evolving towards that state.

Categories of non-liberated soul

Ekendriya - beings with one sense

Jains include many things as jivas that non-Jains regard as either inanimate or plants. They classify these as immobile beings, with only one sense - the sense of touch:

- Earth-bodied: clay, sand, metal, etc
- Water-bodied: fog, rain, ice, etc
- Fire-bodied: fire, lightning, etc
- Air-bodied: wind, gas, etc
- Plant-bodied: trees, flowers, vegetables, etc

Beindriya – beings with two senses

These are very simple organisms that are thought to have two senses - touch and taste. This category includes things like worms and termites.

Treindriya – beings with three senses

These have the senses of touch, taste, and smell. This category includes insects like ants, beetles, and moths.

Chaurindriya – beings with four senses

These have the senses of touch, taste, smell, and sight. This category includes wasps, locusts and scorpions.

Panchendriya – beings with five senses

These have the senses of touch, taste, smell, sight, and hearing. There are four classes of these beings:

- Infernal beings: souls living in hell. This form of jiva experiences the greatest suffering.
- Higher animals: This includes all non-human animals above insects.
- Human beings: This is the only form of jiva

which is able to obtain liberation directly.
- Heavenly beings: This form of the jiva is the happiest.

Five

PRACTICES OF JAINISM

Svetambara monks are allowed to retain a few possessions such as a robe, an alms bowl, a whisk broom, and a *mukhavastrika* (a piece of cloth held over the mouth to protect against the ingestion of small insects), which are presented by a senior monk at the time of initiation. For the non-image-worshiping Sthanakvasi and the Terapanthis, the *mukhavastrika* must be worn at all times. After initiation a monk must adhere to the "great vows" (*mahavratas*) to avoid injuring any life-form, lying, stealing, having sexual intercourse, or accepting personal possessions. To help him keep his vows, a monk's life is carefully regulated in all details by specific ordinances and by the oversight of his superiors. For example, to help him observe the

17

vow of nonviolence, a monk may not take his simple, vegetarian meals after dark, because to do so would increase the possibility of harming insects that might be attracted to the food. In addition, drinking water must first be boiled to ensure that there are no life-forms in it. Monks are expected to suffer from equanimity hardships imposed by the weather, geographic terrain, travel, or physical abuse; however, exceptions are allowed in emergencies, since a monk who survives a calamity can purify himself by confession and by practicing even more rigorous austerities.

Digambara monks take the same "great vows" as do the Shvetambara, but, in acknowledgment of a much more intense interpretation of the vow of non possession, full-fledged Digambara monks remain naked, while lower-grade Digambara monks wear a loincloth and keep with them one piece of cloth not more than 1.5 yards (1.4 meters) long. Digambara monks use a peacock-feather duster to sweep the ground where they walk to avoid injuring any life-forms and drink water from a gourd. They beg for their only meal of the day using the cupped palms of their hand as an alms bowl. They regard their interpretation of the Jain monastic vocation as more in accord with the ancient model than that followed by the Svetambaras.

All Jain renunciations must exercise the three

*Gupti*s (care in thought, speech, and action) and the five *samiti*s (types of vigilance over conduct). Essential to regular monastic ritual are the six "obligatory actions" (*avashyakta*), practiced daily and at important times of the ritual calendar: equanimity (*samayika*, a form of contemplative activity, which, in theory operates throughout the monk's entire career); praise of the Tirthankaras; obeisance to the Tirthankaras, teachers, and scriptures; confession; resolution to avoid sinful activities; and "abandonment of the body" (standing or sitting in a meditative posture).

The type of austerities in which a monk engages, the length of time he practices them, and their severity are carefully regulated by his preceptor, who takes into account the monk's spiritual development, his capacity to withstand the austerities, and his ability to understand how they help further his spiritual progress. The theoretical culmination of a monk's ascetic rigor is the act of *sallekhana*, in which he lies on one side on a bed of thorny grass and ceases to move or eat. This act of ritual starvation is the monk's ultimate act of nonattendance, by which he lets go of the body for the sake of his soul. Jain ideology views this as the ultimate act of self-control and triumph over the passions, rather than simply as suicide. While widely followed in ancient and medieval times, *sallekhana* is much less common today.

Both the Svetambaras and Digambaras allow the initiation of nuns, and among the Svetambaras nuns outnumber monks by a ratio of approximately 3 to 1. Nevertheless, the status of Jain nuns is less prestigious than that of monks, to whom they are obliged by convention and textual stipulation to defer, despite the fact that these nuns are often women of great learning and spiritual attainment. In Digambara Jainism, nuns, who wear robes, accept the necessity of being reborn as men before they can advance significantly on the ascetic path.

The religious activity of the laity

While Jain literature from the earliest times emphasizes the place of the monk and his concerns, it is clear that almost from the religion's outset the majority of Jain's have been laypersons who support the community of renunciations. The medieval period was a time of particularly intense reflection by both Svetambara and Digambara monks on the role of the laity. Many treatises discussing the layman's religious behavior and vows were produced between the 5th and 17th century. According to these writings, lay behavior should mirror the ascetic "great vows." Jain doctrine, however, holds that while the ascetic path can lead to the destruction (*Mirjana*) of karma, the lay path allows only for the warding off (*samvara*) of new karma and thus does not radically alter an individual's karmic status.

The layman (Jainism's focus is invariably upon the male) is enjoined to observe eight basic rules of behavior, which vary but usually include the avoidance of night eating, as well as a diet that excludes meat, wine, honey, and types of fruits and roots deemed to harbor life-forms. There are also 12 vows to be taken: five *anuvratas* ("little vows"), three *gunavratas*, and four *Shiksha vratas*. The *anuvratas* are vows to abstain from violence, falsehood, and stealing; to be content with one's own wife, and to limit one's possessions. The other vows are supplementary and meant to strengthen and protect the *anuvratas*. They involve avoidance of unnecessary travel, of harmful activities, and of the pursuit of pleasure; fasting and control of diet; offering gifts and service to monks, the poor, and fellow believers; and voluntary death if the observance of the major vows proves impossible.

Lay people are further enjoined to perform the six "obligatory actions" at regular intervals, especially the *samayika*, a meditative and renunciatory ritual of limited duration. This ritual is intended to strengthen the resolve to pursue the spiritual discipline of Jain dharma (moral virtue) and is thought to bring the lay votary close to the demands required of an ascetic. It may be performed at home, in a temple, in a fasting hall, or before a monk.

Dating from early in the history of Jainism are 11 stages of a layman's spiritual progress, or *Pratima* ("statue"). Medieval writers conceived *Pratima* as a ladder leading to higher stages of spiritual development. The last two stages lead logically to the renunciation of the world and the assumption of the ascetic life.

It was natural for monastic legislators to portray the careers of idealized laypeople as a preparatory stage to the rigors of ascetic life, but for Jain lay life to have meaning it need not necessarily culminate in initiation as a monk. With its careful rules about food, its regular ceremonies, and cultural traditions, Jainism provides the laity a rounded social world. Typically, Jain lay life is character- ized by strict vegetarianism, disciplined business or professional activity, and responsible conduct of family affairs with a view to establishing a sound social reputation. Lay Jains believe that pious activity including fasting and almsgiving, and especially the practice of nonviolence enables an individual not only to advance a little further along the path to final liberation but to improve his current material situation. As a result, there is a stark contrast between the great prosperity of the

Jain lay community and the austere self-denial of the monks and nuns it supports.

Until very recently Jainism had not developed any distinctive life-cycle rituals for events such as birth and marriage, although in the 9th century the Digambara monk Jinasena attempted to legislate in this area. In general, the practice has tended to conform to prevailing local customs, provided this does not infringe on basic Jain principles.

Image veneration

Temple worship is mentioned in early texts that describe god's paying homage to images and relics of Tirthankaras in heavenly eternal shrines. While Mahavira himself appears to have made no statement regarding image veneration, it quickly became a vital part of the Jain tradition. Numerous images of Tirthankaras in the sitting and standing postures dating from the early Common Era have been uncovered in excavations of a Jain stupa, or funerary monument, at Mathura in Uttar Pradesh. The earliest images of Tirthankaras are all nude and distinguished by carved inscriptions of their names on the pedestals. By the 5th century, symbols specific to each Tirthankara (e.g., a lion for Mahavira) began to appear. The practice of associating one of the 24 *shasanadevatas* ("doctrine goddesses") with images of individual Tirthankaras began in the 9th century. Some of these goddesses, such as Ambika ("Little Mother"), who is associated with the Tirthankara Arishtanemi, continue to have great importance for the Jain devotee. The images are generally located near the entrance to Jain temples and can be propitiated for aid in worldly matters.

Closely associated with the obligatory rites of the laity, worship (*puja*) can be made to all liberated souls, to monks, and to the scriptures. The focus for most image-venerating Jains (*murtipujak*) is the icon of the Tirthankara located in the central shrine room of the temple or, alternatively, in a domestic shrine. Temples also house subsidiary Tirthankara images. Although Tirthankaras remain unaffected by offerings and worship and cannot, as individuals who are liberated from rebirth, respond in any way, such devotional actions serve as a form of a meditative discipline. Daily worship includes hymns of praise and prayers, the recitation of sacred formulas and the names of the Tirthankaras, and idol veneration bathing the image and making offerings to it of flowers, fruit, and rice. Sve-tambaras also decorate images with clothing and ornaments. A long-standing debate within both Jain communities concerns the relative value of external acts of worship and internalized acts of mental discipline and meditation. Monks and nuns of all sects are prohibited from displays of physical worship.

Festivals

Important days in the Jain calendar are called parvan, and on these days religious observances, such as structured periods of fasting and festivals, take place. The principal Jain festivals can generally be connected with the five major events in the life of each Tirthankara: descent into his mother's womb, birth, renunciation, attainment of omniscience, and final emancipation.

The Jain calendar includes many festivals. Among them is the Shvetambara fasting ceremony, *oli*, which is celebrated for nine days twice a year (in March–April and September–October) and which corresponds to the mythical celestial worship of the images of the Tirthankaras. The most significant time of the Jain ritual year, however, is the four-month period, generally running from late July to early November, when monks and nuns abandon the wandering life and live in the midst of lay communities. For Svetambaras, the single most important festival, Paryushana, occurs in the month of Bhadrapada (August–September). *Paryushana* ("Abiding") designates, on the one hand, pacification by forgiving and service with wholehearted effort

25

and devotion and, on the other, staying at one place for the monsoon season. The festival is characterized by fasting, preaching, and scriptural recitation. On its last day, Samvatsari ("Annual"), alms are distributed to the poor, and a Jina image is ceremonially paraded through the streets. A communal confession is performed by the laity, and letters are sent asking for forgiveness and the removal of all ill feelings about conscious or unconscious misdeeds during the past year. The equivalent Digambara festival is called Dashalak-shanaparvan ("Observance Day of the 10 Religious Qualities") and centers on the public display of an important text, the *Tattvartha-sutra*.

On the full-moon day of the month of Kartika (October–November), at the same time that Hindus celebrate Diwali (the festival of lights), Jains commemorate the nirvana (final liberation; literally "becoming extinguished") of Mahavira by lighting lamps. Another important Shvetambara ceremony, Jnana Panchami (literally "Knowledge Fifth," where "Fifth" signifies a date), occurs five days later and is celebrated with temple worship and with reverence of the scriptures. The equivalent Digambara festival takes place in May–June. Mahavir Jayanti, the birthday of Mahavira, is celebrated by both sects in early April with public processions.

The most famous of all Jain festivals, Mastakabhisheka ("Head Anointment"), is performed every 12 years at the Digambara sacred complex at Shravanabelagola ("White Lake of the Ascetics") in Karnataka state. In this ceremony, the 57-foot- (17-metre-) high statue of Bahubali is anointed from above with a variety of substances (water, milk, flowers, etc.) in the presence of an audience that can approach one million.

Pilgrimage

Pilgrimage, viewed as a particularly meritorious activity, is popular among renunciations and laity alike. Places of pilgrimage were created during the medieval period at sites marking the principal events in the lives of Tirthankaras, some of which were destroyed during the Muslim invasions, which started in the 8th century. Parasnath Hill and Rajgir in Bihar state and Shatrunjaya and Girnar hills on the Kathiawar Peninsula are among such important ancient pilgrimage sites. Other shrines that have become pilgrimage destinations are Shravanabelagola in Karnataka state, Mounts Abu and Kesariyaji in Rajasthan state, and Antariksha Parshvanatha in Akola district of Maharashtra. For those unable to go on pilgrimage to the most famous sites, it is possible to worship their depictions in local temples. Small regional networks of shrines are also regarded as simulacra of the great pilgrimage sites.

Six

RITUALS OF JAINISM

Sacred Time

Jain time is cyclical, moving through stages in which dharma grows progressively weaker and conditions in karma-bhumi deteriorate accordingly. Each of these cycles is marked by the return of the twenty-four Tirthankaras, who eternally refresh Jain Dharma through their identical teachings.

Sacred Space

Some Jain sects do not build temples, as they consider their construction and use to be a violent attachment. For Jain's who do attend temples, there are many important pilgrimage sites in India considered to be sources of spiritual power. Some Jain sects do not build temples, as they consider their construction and use to be a violent attachment. For Jain's who do attend temples, there are many important pilgrimage sites in India considered to be sources of spiritual power.

Jainism Rites and Ceremonies

Rituals differ by sect, but generally include fasts, devotional worship, and meditation. Initiation into renunciation orders is effected by the elaborate Diksha ritual. The ritual of Sallekhana entails fasting until death when one's body begins to interfere with spiritual progress.

Worship and Devotion in Daily Life

Rituals differ by sect, but generally include fasts, devotional worship, and meditation. Initiation into renunciation orders is effected by the elaborate Diksha ritual. The ritual of Sallekhana entails fasting until death when one's body begins to interfere with spiritual progress.

Symbolism

The official symbol of Jainism is a pictograph whose geometric outline symbolizes the world (lok); within the image is a raised hand inscribed with "ahimsa" (non- violence); a swastika symbolizing the four worlds into which one can be reborn; three dots symbolizing the three jewels of Jainism; and an arc symbolizing the abode of the Siddhas.

Seven

WHAT IS KARMA ?

Karma is the mechanism that determines the quality of life. The happiness of a being's present life is the result of the moral quality of the actions of the being in its previous life.

A soul can only achieve liberation by getting rid of all the karma attached to it.

Karma is a logical and understandable way of making sense of good and evil, the different qualities of different lives and the different moral status of different types of creatures, without having to involve rules laid down by a god.

Karma works without the intervention of any other being - gods or angels have no part to play in dispensing rewards or punishments.

Karma is a concept found in religions which

32

include reincarnation in their beliefs. Different religions have different ideas as to exactly how karma operates.

The Jain idea of karma is much more elaborate and mechanistic than that found in some other Eastern religions.

Karma is a physical substance

Jains believe that karma is a physical substance that is everywhere in the universe. Karma particles are attracted to the jiva (soul) by the actions of that jiva.

It may be helpful to think of karma as floating dust which sticks to the soul, or as types of atomic particle which are attracted to the soul as a result of our actions, words, and thoughts. On their own, karma particles have no effect but when they stick to a soul they affect the life of that soul.

We attract karma particles when we do or think or say things: we attract karma particles if we kill something, we attract karma particles when we tell a lie, we attract karma particles when we steal and so on.

The quantity and nature of the karma particles sticking to the soul cause the soul to be happy or unhappy and affect the events in the soul's present and future lives.

It's a compound process in that the accumulation

of karma causes us to have bad thoughts, deeds, emotions and vices, and these bad actions (etc) cause our souls to attract more karma, which causes more bad thoughts, and so on.

Avoiding and removing karma

Karma can be avoided in two ways

- By behaving well - so no karma is attracted
- By having the right mental state - so that even if an action attracts karma, the correct mental attitude of the being means that karma either doesn't stick to that soul or is discharged immediately

Some karma expires on their own after causing suffering. Other karmas remain. The karma that has built up on the soul can be removed by living life according to the Jain vows.

Outline of karma

- Karma is a physical substance
- This substance is everywhere in the universe
- There are 8 forms of karma
- The mental, verbal and physical actions of the jiva attract karma to it. The more intense the

activity, the more karma is attracted

- The karma sticks to the jiva because negative characteristics of the jiva, passions like anger, pride and greed, make the jiva sticky. Karma can be warded off by avoiding these negative characteristics
- If the being is without passions then the karma does not stick, thus a person can avoid karma sticking to them by leading a religiously correct life
- Karma must be burned off the jiva in order for it to make spiritual progress. Living according to the Jain vows is the way to get rid of karma
- The jiva takes its karma with it from one life to another

The 8 types of karma

These types of karma can be split equally into destructive and non-destructive karma.

Destructive karma's

- mohaniya-karma (delusory):
- deludes the jiva
- causes attachment to false beliefs
- prevents the jiva from living a correct life
- jnana-avaraniya-karma (knowledge-obscuring):

- interferes with the jiva's intellect and senses
- prevents the jiva from understanding the truth
- blocks the jiva's natural omniscience
- dars(h)an-avarniya-karma (perception-obscuring):
- interferes with perception through the senses
- antaraya-karma (obstructing):
- obstructs the energy of the jiva
- blocks the doing of good acts that the jiva wants to do

Non-destructive karmas

- vedaniya-karma (feeling-producing):
- determines whether the jiva has pleasant or unpleasant experiences
- Nama-karma (physique-determining):
- determines the type of rebirth
- determines the physical characteristics of the new life
- determines the spiritual potential of the new life
- ayu-karma (life-span-determining):
- determines the duration of a being's life (within the limits of the species into which the jiva is reborn)
- gotra-karma (status-determining):
- determines the status of a being within its species.

Eight

JAINISM IN THE MODERN ERA

Followers of the path practiced by the Jinas are known as Jains. The majority of Jains currently reside in India. With four to five million followers worldwide, Jainism is relatively small compared to major world religions. Jain communities can be found in Europe, the United States, Canada, and Kenya.

According to the National Family and Health Survey conducted in 2015-16, Jains form the wealthiest community in India. Jains have the highest literacy rate (87%) in India, in the 7-years to oldest age group, according to its 2011 census. The Jaina community also has the highest number of college graduates. Excluding the retired senior citizens, the

Jain literacy rate in India exceeded 97%. Further,
Jain males have the highest work participation rates.

Nine

LIFE OF AN JAIN MONK!

when a person renounces the worldly life and all the attachments and is initiated into monkshood or nunhood, the man is called Sadhu, Shraman or Muni and the woman is called Sadhvi, Shramani, or Aryï. Their renunciation is total which means they are completely detached from the social and worldly activities and they do not take any part in those activities anymore. Instead, they spend their time spiritual uplifting their souls and guiding householders such as ourselves how to uplift our souls.

When they get initiated into the life of Sadhus and Sadhvis, they take five major vows and act strictly following those vows. The five great vows are:

1) **Pranatipitaviraman Mahavrat** - Vow of ab-

solute Non-violence.

The first vow of Pranatipï Taviramany Mahavrat means sadhu and sadhvis will never cause harm or violence to any living being including even the tiniest creatures.

2) **Mrishavadaviraman Mahïvrat** - Vow of absolute Truthfulness

The second vow of Mrishavadaviraman Mahïvrat means they will not lie.

3) **Adattadinaviraman Mahavrat** - Vow of absolute Non-stealing

The third vow of Adattadinaviraman Mahavrat means without the permission of the owner they will not take anything from anywhere.

4) **Maithuna Viraman Mahavrat** - Vow of absolute Celibacy

The fourth vow of Maithuna Viraman Mahavrat means they have to observe the celibacy with absolute adherence to it. The sadhu or sadhvis should not even touch a member of the opposite sex regardless of their age.

5) **Parigraha Viraman Mahavrat** - Vow of absolute Non-attachment.

The fifth vow of Parigraha Viraman Mahavrat means they do not possess anything and do not have any attachment for things they keep for their daily needs.

In summary, while taking these vows, they say, "O

Lord Arihant! I will not commit the sins of violence, express falsehood, steal and enjoy sensual pleasures, or be possessive, by speech, thought or deed; nor will I assist or order anyone to commit these sins. I will not approve or endorse anyone committing such sins. Oh, Lord! I hereby take a sacred and solemn vow that throughout my life, I will follow these five major vows and strictly follow the code of conduct laid out for a sadhu and a sadhvi."

Therefore, Jain Sadhus and Sadhvis never cause harm or violence to any living being. They live according to the pledge that they do not harm even the tiniest creatures. They always speak the absolute truth. They do not lie on account of fear, desire, anger or deceptive intentions. Without the permission of the owner, they do not take even the smallest thing such as a straw. They observe the vow of celibacy with absolute adherence to it. They will not touch the members of the opposite sex, even a child. In case the members of the opposite sex either touch them by mistake or in ignorance, they have to undergo the ritual of repentance (Prayaschitta) for self-purification. Jain Sadhus should not keep money with them. They will not own or have any control over any wealth, houses, any such movable or immovable property or organization. They will limit their necessities to the lowest limit and apart from these limits they should not have any attachments.

Some special rules of conduct for sadhus and sadhvis:

The Jain sadhus or sadhvis do not take food or water after the sunset or before sunrise. They wait 48 minutes after the sun-rise before even drinking boiled water. Under any circumstance, they do not eat or drink anything between the hours of sunset and sunrise.

Gochari (Alm): Jain sadhus/sadhvis do not cook their food, do not get it prepared for them, or do not accept any food which was prepared for them. They go to different householders that are Jains or vegetarians and receive a little food from each house. This practice is called Gochari. Just as cows graze the top part of grass moving from place to place, taking a little at one place and a little at another, in the same way, Jain Monks and Nuns do not take all the food from one house. They collect it from various houses. The reason Jain Sadhus/sadhvis accept a little food and not all the food from one house is that this way the householders do not have to cook again. The cooking process involves much violence in the form of fire, vegetable chopping, water consumption, etc., and sadhus or sadhvis do not want to be part of any violence due to their needs. They do not receive food standing outside the house, but they go inside the house where food is cooked or kept. This way they can understand the situation that their accepting food would not make the householders cook again. They accept food which is within the limit of their vows.

Vihar: They always walk with bare feet. When they travel from one place to another, whatever may be the distance they always go walking. They do not use any vehicle like bullock cart, car, boat, ship or plane for traveling. Whether it is cold weather or scorching sun; whether the road is stony or thorny; whether it is the burning sand of a desert or a burning road, they do not wear any foot-wear at any time. They move about barefoot all their life. The reason for not wearing shoes is while walking, they can avoid crushing the bugs or insects on the ground. While going places, they preach the religion (Dharma) and provide proper spiritual guidance to people. They do not stay more than a few days in any one place except during the rainy season which is about four months in duration. The sadhus and sadhvis generally do not go out at night. The place where they stay is called Upashray or Parishad Shala. They may stay in places other than the Upashrayas if those places are suitable for the practice of their disciplined life and if they do not disturb or impede the code of conduct. The reason they do not stay anywhere permanently or for a longer period in one place is to avoid

43

developing attachment for material things and the people around them.

Loch: The Jain Sï¿½dhus and Sadhvis after receiving the Diksha (initiation) do not cut their hair or shave their heads; nor do they get these things done by a barber. But twice a year or at least once a year at the time of Paryushan, they pluck off their hairs or they get the hairs plucked by others. This is called Kesh Lochan or Loch. This way they are not dependent on others to carry out their needs. It is also considered as one kind of austerity where one bears the pain of plucking off the hairs calmly.

Clothing: They always wear un-stitched or minimally stitched white clothes. Some Jain sadhus do not wear clothes. A loincloth that reaches up to the shins is called a Cholapattak. Another cloth to cover the upper part of the body is called Pangarani (Uttariya Vastra). A cloth that passes over the left shoulder and covers the body up to a little above the ankle is called a Kï¿½mli. Kï¿½mli is a woolen shawl. They also carry a woolen bed sheet and a woolen mat to sit on. Those who wear clothes have a muhapatti a square or rectangular piece of cloth of a prescribed measurement either in their hand or tied on their face covering the mouth. They also have Ogho or Rajoharan (a broom of woolen threads) to clean insects around their sitting place or while they are walking. Sadhus who do not wear any clothes have morpichhi and kamandal in their hands. These are the articles by which they can be distinguished. This practice may vary among different sects of Jains but the essential principle remains the same to limit needs.

They bestow their blessings on all, uttering the words Dharm Labh (may you attain spiritual prosperity). They bless everyone alike irrespective of their caste, creed. sex, age, wealth, poverty, high, or low social status. Some put Vakshep (scented sandal dust) on the heads of people. Monks and nuns show the path of wholesome life and righteous and disciplined life to everyone through the media of discussions, discourses, seminars, and camps to attain spiritual prosperity.

The entire life of sadhus/sadhvis is directed towards the welfare of their souls. All the activities of their life have only one aim, namely, self-purification for self- realization. For the attainment of this objective, besides following laid down guidelines they perform the pratikraman daily and perform other austerities.

Conferring a title:

The Jain sadhus, after being initiated that is, after receiving the Diksha becomes immersed in such activities as meditation, seeking knowledge, acquiring self-discipline, etc. Proceeding on the path of spiritual endeavor, when they reach a higher level of attainment, their spiritual elders, for the preservation of the four-fold Jain Sangh, confer upon them some special titles.

The Title of Acharya: This title is considered to be very high and involves a great responsibility. The entire responsibility of the Jain Sangh rests on the shoulders of the acharya. Before attaining this title, one has to make an in-depth study and a thorough exploration of the Jain Agamas and attain mastery of them. One must also study the various languages of the surrounding territory and have acquired a thorough knowledge of all the philosophies of the world related to different ideologies and religions.

The Title of Upadhyay: This title is given to a sadhu who teaches all the sadhus and sadhvis, and has acquired a specialized knowledge of the Agams (Scriptures).

The Title of Panya's and Gani: To secure this title, one should have acquired an in-depth knowledge of all the Jain agams. To attain the status of Ganipad one should know about the Bhagavati Sutra and to attain the Panyas-pad one should have attained comprehensive knowledge of all the aspects of the agams.

The Jain sadhus, on account of the mode of their life, are unique among all the monks. The entire life of Sadhus and Sadhvis is dedicated to the spiritual welfare of their souls; all their objectives, and all their activities are directed towards elevating their souls to the Paramatma-dasha, the state of the Supreme Soul.

The above description is related to Svetambara Monks.

The main concept of renunciation is the same in both the Shwetambar and Digambar sections. But there are some differences in what they keep and how they take Gochari/Ahar. Digambar monks do not wear any clothes. Elak was one cloth. Kulak wears two clothes. Digambar Nuns wear white clothes. All of them keep keeping Morpichhi and Kamandal. All of them eat once a day from "Choka". These chokas are arranged by Householders and they invite Monks and nuns to accept the food from there. Digambar monks and elaks eat standing up and in their hands. Kulaks eat in one utensil. Nuns eat in their hands or the utensil.

Ten

ORIGINS

Jainism is one of the oldest religions of India. We do not know exactly when it was founded. The Jain's themselves say that Jainism has existed since eternity and it had like the Jain universe no beginning and would have no end. Most of the saints of Jainism belonged to remote ages, millions and billions of years ago. However, for practical purposes, we may take Mahavira, their last great saint, as a historical figure. He was a contemporary of the Buddha.

Mahavira was the twenty-fourth and last of the Tirthankara (ford-makers) of this age. The twenty-third Tirthankara was Parshvanatha. He is said to have lived two hundred and fifty years before Mahavira. The historicity of Mahavira is difficult to prove from Jain sources alone because these were reduced to writing quite late. One of the two main sects of the Jain's, the Digambaras think that no records of the period of Mahavira have survived. The other sect, the Svetambaras assert that the oral traditions of the time of Mahavira were put down in the written form in the fifth century AD, i.e., a thousand years after Mahavira. Some account of the life of Mahavira can be obtained from this literature. According to the Svetambaras, Mahavira was born in Vaishali a place about 45 km. from Patna on Chaitra, Shukla Trayodashi in 599 BC. He was the Kshatriya prince belonging to the Jnatra clan. He died in 527 BC in Pavapuri near Rajagriha. King Shrenika and his son Kunika were the rulers of Magadha during his time.

The historicity of Mahavira is sought to be proved by comparing these facts with those obtained from the Buddhist sources. The Pali Buddhist texts on the life and sayings of the Buddha are claimed to have been compiled shortly after his death. They mention quite often a Nataputta who belonged to the sect of the Niganthas (free from bonds.) According to these sources, Nataputta died in Pava thirty years before the death of the Buddha. The rulers of Magadh during the Buddha's time were Bimbisara and his son Ajatashatru.

It is asserted that the person mentioned as Nataputta in the Buddhist texts was the same as Mahavira, the Jnatraputra of the Jains. The name of the place where he died is the same in both the sets of sources. Shrenika and Kunika, the two kings mentioned in the Jain sources were Bimbisara and Ajatashatru mentioned in the Buddhist (as well as in the Hindu Purana) texts. The full name Shrenika Bimbisara is mentioned in the (Jain) Dasasruta Skandha.

Ajatashatru's son according to the Buddhist sources was Udayabhadra. According to the Jain sources Kunika's son was Udayin. Since the names of the sons also are similar Kunika is identified with Ajatashatru.

Jain, as the name of this particular sect, does not occur in the Buddhist sources. The reason is that both Mahavira and the Buddha were called Jina by their respective followers, and the term Jain would thus technically denote both the sects. However, the Niganthas according to the Buddhists were known for extreme asceticism. This is a characteristic, which differentiates the Buddhists and the Jains. There is little doubt, therefore, that the Niganthas are the same people who were known as the Jains in later days. The old Jain literature such as the Acharanga Sutra and the Kalpa Sutra describe their community as that of Nigganthas.

However, the historicity of Mahavira is not cru-

cial to the history of Jainism. Mahavira was not
the founder of Jainism in the sense that the Buddha
was the founder of Buddhism. As stated earlier the
Jains claim that their religion had existed from time
immemorial, and Mahavira was the last great saint
and reformer of the religion. The most important of
these reforms was the introduction of five vows in
place of the four obtaining in the system of Parshva
(the twenty-third Tirthankara of the Jains).

The later history of Jainism is marked by several
schisms. But one might say that different groups existed among the Jains even at the time of Mahavira
himself. There was an ascetic called Keshi who
followed the system of Parshvanatha. He had a long
discussion with Gautama, a disciple of Mahavira,
and finally accepted the latter's views and sincerely
adopted the "Law of the five vows". Thus Parshva
group and Mahavira's group, originally separate,
were united. However, new schisms appeared according to the Svetambaras, even during Mahavira's
lifetime. The first schism was by his son-in-law
Jamali 14 years after Mahavira's enlightenment.
The various schisms are known as nihnavas.

The most important schism, the eighth nihnava
according to the Svetambaras, occurred among
the Jains a few centuries after Mahavira. At that
time the community broke into the two sects, the
Digambaras (the skyclad) and Svetambaras (the

white-robed). It is interesting to note that the two sects describe the life of Mahavira differently. The Svetambaras say that Mahavira lived as a prince up to the age of thirty. He had married and had a daughter, Anojja or Priyadarshana. His granddaughter Yashomati was born after Mahavira had left home. Digambaras, on the other hand, believe that Mahavira never married.

Before we come to the difference among the sects, we may consider the basic religious philosophy of the Jains. These are practically the same for both the sects and have remained almost unchanged from very early times.

"According to Jain philosophy, matter, which consists of atoms, is eternal but may assume any form, such as earth, wind, and so on. All material things are ultimately produced by a combination of atoms. Souls are of two kinds: those, which are subject to mundane transmigration (samsaric), and those, which are liberated (Mukta). The latter will be embodied no more they dwell in a state of perfection at the summit of the universe; being no more concerned with worldly affairs they have reached Nirvana."

The souls (Jiva) with which the whole world is filled are different from matter; But being substances they are also eternal. Subtle matter coming into contact with the soul causes its embodiment;

being then transformed into eight kinds of karma and thus forming as it were a subtle body, it clings (ashrava) to the soul in all its migrations. The theory of karma is the keystone of the Jain system. The highest goal consists in getting rid (nirjara) of all karma derived from past existences and acquiring no new karma (samvara). One of the chief means of this end is the performance of asceticism (topas). The Jain system differs from Buddhism in emphasizing asceticism to a greater extent, even to the point of religious suicide: and in the total evidence of taking the life of any kind, such avoidance being described as the highest duty.

The methods by which a Jain could get rid of the acquired karma and attain Nirvana have been prescribed. He should possess the right faith, right knowledge, and right conduct. These are called tri-Ratna. He should also observe the following five vows:

1) Ahinsa (non-killing).
2) Sunrita (truthful speech).
3) Asteya (non-stealing).
4) Brahmacharya (celibacy), and
5) Aparigraha (non-possession).

As mentioned earlier Parshvanatha had prescribed only four vows. Mahavira splits Parshvanatha's fourth vow, which was perhaps Aparigraha into two. It is said that Brahmacharya was already included in Aparigraha, but Mahavira made it explicit to remove any misunderstanding.

These vows are difficult for a layman to practice. Laymen were, therefore, required to observe these vows to the extent permitted by the conditions of their lives.

It will be noticed at once that the Jain point of view of human life and its end are completely different from the Vedic ideals. There is no mention of transmigration of the soul or the theory of karma or Nirvana in the Rigveda. The Vedic view of life is joyful. The Vedas prescribe the performance of Yoga, where animals were sacrificed. These were done to please the gods and also for taking the sacrificer to paradise after his death. The paradise itself was a delightful place where there was no death. Vedic heaven was full of light and all desires were fulfilled there. Drinking of Soma (perhaps as an intoxicant) was a method of gaining all desirable objects on the earth. There is no thought in the Vedas of ascetic life while on earth.7 The Vedas envisage a priestly class who would correctly recite the Vedic hymns at the time of the sacrifices. The Jains on the other hand neither have any hymns nor have any priestly class of their own. Indeed it is specifically mentioned that their great saints, the Tirthankara, were Kshatriyas i.e., not Brahmans. Similarly, meditation (yoga), the atomic theory of

54

matter (Vaisheshika), the non- perishing of matter (Sankhya), etc., would take the Jain thinking nearer of those systems of Indian philosophy which are not based on the Vedas. It is also interesting to note that Kapil, Kanda, etc., the founders of these non-Vedic systems were known as Tairthikas. There were eighteen or more Tairthikas according to the encyclopedists. The similarity of this name with Tairthikas is striking. (Strangely enough, the Buddhists also called those who held heretical views, Tairthikas.)

Mahavira, and to some extent the Buddha, ignores the existence of the Vedic religion. When in their youth they left their homes to become ascetics they are not protesting against any Vedic or Brahmin rule. It appears that they were doing just what was thought proper for a person of a religious bent of mind in that part of the country. The Buddha after trying it abandoned the extreme form of asceticism. Thus, he was reacting against the practices followed by the Jains and similar other ascetics, when he founded his new faith of moderation.

An important thing about Buddhism and Jainism is that their religions are not much concerned about-worldly things. Also, they have no theistic theories. Present-day Hinduism, on the other hand, is much preoccupied with these things. Signs of emergence among a section of the people of such thoughts become apparent in the post-Vedic literature such as Upanishads. These show that a new post-Vedic religion was emerging. The Brihadaranyaka Upanishad is one of the earliest of the Upanishads. It was perhaps compiled within a hundred years of the time when the Buddha and Mahavira lived. Some of the dialogues in this Upanishad took place in Videha (modern Mithila) which is not very far from Magadh where these two great teachers preached. Thus both in time and space, the two ages, the Upanishad and the Buddhist-Janis, are not far from each other. Yet, one feels that they belong to two different worlds together. We may as an example take the questions the king Janak of Videha asked Yajnavalkya in the Brihadaranyaka Upanishad:

Janak Vaidehi said: "When the sun has set, O Yajnavalkya and the moon has set, and the fire is gone out, and the sound hushed, what is then the light of man".

Yajnavalkya said: "The Self indeed is his light; for having the Self alone as his light, the man sits, moves about, does his work, and returns."

Janak Vaidehi said: "Who is that Self?"

Yajnavalkya replied: "He who is within the heart, surrounded by the pranas

(senses), the person of light, consisting of knowledge…..."

It is quite clear that the questions, as well as the answers, are otherworldlyy. They do not relate to any human activity.

As a contrast, we may cite the question in which king Ajatashatru of Magadh asked six of the non-Vedic teachers preaching at that time in his kingdom. One of the teachers was Mahavira (Nigantha Nataputta) himself.

The question King Ajatashatru of Magadh asked, was, "The fruits of various worldly trades and professions are obvious, but is it possible to show any appreciable benefit to be derived from asceticism? Sanditthikam samanna-phalam?" Each of the six teachers gave a different answer. These answers need not concern us at the moment. The point, however, to notice is that the question is quite mundane and very natural for a king, but it is in a different plane altogether from the one king Janak of Videha has asked. We may thus take it as a working hypothesis that we are here dealing with two communities, one non-Vedic and the other post-Vedic whose outlooks were altogether different. The Buddhist scriptures name sixteen tribes living in northern India at that time. The land where they lived was also named after the tribes. Of these tribes, the Kurus, the Panchalas, the Machchas, the Saurasena, etc., followed the post-Vedic and

Brahmanic religion. The people before whom the Buddha preached, his new religion or one of whose existing religions Mahavira reformed were the Magadh, the Angas, the Kasihs, the Koalas,10 the Mallas, the Vajjis, etc. The religions of these people were non- Vedic. There is one initial difficulty in this hypothesis. the Vajjis included eight confederate clans, of whom the Lichchhavis and the Videhas were the most important. Videha, in Buddha's time, was the republic. This does not go very well with the fact that Janak was the king of Videha or with the fact that he followed a Brahmanic or post-Vedic religion. Perhaps by Buddha's time, Videha had become a republic. One way of getting out of the second difficulty would be to imagine that in Videha both the groups of religions, post-Vedic and non- Vedic existed side by side. This was perhaps also true of Kashi and Kosala, where also both the communities visited the areas, people of his group would flock about him while the other groups would ignore him. (The position is the same even today. If a Hindu religious teacher visits a town his followers go and greet him but the Muslims are not even aware of his visit).

The people of Anga (Bhagalpur area) and the Magadh Patna, Gaya, area) do not seem to have followed the Vedic religion, for they were very much disliked by the Vedic people. We have the curse in the Atharva Veda (V. 22.14): "To the Gand-hari's, the Mujavants, the Anga, the Magadh, like one sending a person a treasure, do we commit the fever". The Vedic people called the Aryans who did not follow their religions Vratyas. Vratyas are frequently mentioned in the Vedas and other Vedic literature such as the Srauta Sutras and the Brahmans. The whole of the fifteenth book of the Atharva Veda deals with the Vratyas. Unfortunately, the style of this book of the Atharva Veda is not clear and not much information about the beliefs of the Vratyas can be gleaned out of it. One thing, however, is clear. The Magodhas were somehow connected with the Vratyas. We have in the Atharva Veda (XV.2.a) "Of him in the eastern quarter, faith is the harlot, Mitra the Magadh, discernment the garment, etc....." Similarly in the southern quarter, Magadh was the mantra of the Vratya; in the other two-quarters Magadh was the laughter and the thunder of the Vratya. What Magadh means here is not clear. It may mean a resident of Magadh or more probably a bard or a minstrel. The Yajur Veda (XXX. 8) does not look at Vratyas kindly. They are included in the list of victims at the Purushamedha (human sacrifice). The Sutras mention Arahants (saints) and Yaudheyas (warriors) of the Vratyas corresponding to the Brahmanical, Brahman, and Kshatriya. The similarly of the word Arhant with the word Arhat

59

used both for the Buddha and Mahavira by their respective followers is noticeable.

We thus see that in the period under discussion Mahavira was preaching perhaps one of the Vratya religions which were prevalent in that part of India. This religion came to be known as Jainism in later days. Most of the religions in this area advocated an extreme form of asceticism. Gautama, who later became the Buddha, originally joined this mainstream. Apart from some changes in the philosophical principles, Buddha's main modification was that he deprecated the severe asceticism of these religions.

Jain Yoga as also the Yoga of Patanjali is meditation, preferably in a secluded place. We have the Indus valley evidence of the figure of an ascetic sitting in a forest. The figure found on a seal shows a man sitting in a forest surrounded by several animals. The man has a mask with horns. The figure has been variously interpreted as that of Shiva as Pashupati or Shiva as Mahayogi. But there is no doubt that it is a figure of an ascetic either human or divine. Thus the idea of asceticism though foreign to the Vedic people was already existent in India in the protohistoricc period.

The remarkable similarity between the stone statue of a nude man, found in Mohenjodaro and of the statue said to be that of a Tirthankara found in Lohanipur (Bihar) has often been pointed out.13 But the time interval of almost 2500 years would incline one to think that the similarity is accidental.

That Jainism is a continuation of some pre-Vedic religion is not a new theory. G.

C. Pande wrote in 1947, "The anti-ritualistic tendency within the Vedic fold is itself due to the impact of asceticism which antedated the Vedas. Jainism represents a continuation of this pre-Vedic stream, from which Buddhism also springs, though deeply influenced by Vedic thought."14 Similarly, A.L. Basham says, "In the eastern part of the Ganga basin Brahmanism was not so deeply entrenched as in the west and other non- Aryan currents of belief flowed more strongly."15 Basham's point that all these other currents of belief were non-Aryan cannot, however, be maintained. There is scarcely any non-Aryan word in the sacred literature of Jainism. Thus at least one, of these pre-Vedic currents of belief was Indo-Aryan in origin. It existed in India before the Vedic people arrived in eastern India. It has survived to the present day in the form of Jainism. Also, it is not Buddhism and Jainism and other pre-Vedic religions of the eastern Ganga basin which have influenced Vedism and converted that religion into Brahmanism, and then Hinduism. It is from the pre-Vedic religions that Brahmanism has learned all about asceticism, meditation, yoga, the theory of karma, the theory of the transmigration of souls, Nirvana, and finally the pessimistic view of life.

In a somewhat different context Dandekar, has said almost the same thing: "One may, of course, not go to the extreme of asserting that Hinduism turned its back completely on Vedic beliefs and practices, but one has nevertheless to admit that the impact of Vedism on the mythology, ritual, and philosophy of classical Hinduism has been of a superficial nature."16 Dandekar was developing his thesis that " in the long history of Hinduism, ...Vedism occurred more or less like an interlude".

It would thus appear that Jainism and many other religions existed from pre- Vedic times in northern India. Only Jainism remained practically unaffected by the impact of Vedism. The other religions which coalesced to form classical Hinduism were affected by Vedism, albeit, as Dandekar insists, superficially.

Both Buddhism and Jainism were parts of the philosophic atmosphere prevailing in Magadh and the near about areas in the sixth century BC. We can get a feel of this atmosphere from canonical books of the two religions, for, as we know both of them to purport to give accounts of the actual happenings in the lives of the Buddha and Mahavira respectively. The Buddhist works are a little more helpful in this matter because they give generally greater details of the beliefs of the rival sects. Out of these several competing sects two or three, if we include the Ajivikas) religions emerged triumphantly. This was perhaps mainly due to the quality of leadership and the organizing capacity of the Buddha and Mahavira (and Makkhali Gosala in the case of the Ajivikas).

One thing about the religious atmosphere of this period is quite clear. Among the religious people, the most respected ones in those days were the ascetics. An ascetic didn't need to belong to higher castes like the Brahmans or the Kshatriyas. Even a slave would be respected by his erstwhile master if he joined an order and became an ascetic. The Buddha once asked king Ajatashatru of Magadh whether he would ask a slave to come back and serve him again if he heard that the slave had run away and become a recluse.

Ajatashatru answered "Nay rather should we greet him with reverence, and rise from our seat out of deference towards him, and press him to be seated. And we should have robes and bowl, etc.,... and beg him to accept of them".18 An important point to notice here is that the religious order which the slave might have joined did not matter.

No doubt, the advantage was taken by many people of this attitude toward the ascetics. The rulers themselves perhaps took unfair advantage of this general reverence for the ascetics. They used to send spies to the territories of their hostile neighbors in the guise of ascetics. Common people were aware of these deceptions, and if one or two unknown persons garbed as ascetics were seen in any village they were sometimes suspected to be spies. Mahavira in his pre-kevalin days traveled about the country with Makkhali Gosala for six or seven years. Twice they were suspected to be spies and harassed by the villagers. Once they were thrown into a well, but were rescued when they were identified by some female followers of Parshva.

Another important development that was taking place in eastern India at the time was that the Brahmans were trying to establish their supremacy over the other classes. These Kshatriyas of the area were not prepared to concede. The Ambattha Sutta 20 describes the conversation Buddha had with a Brahman named Ambattha. At that time the Buddha was staying in the Koshala country. This was perhaps the western limit of his missionary work.

When Ambattha came in the presence of the Buddha he behaved in an off-hand manner. The Buddha pulled him up for being discourteous to an aged teacher. Ambattha then complained, "That, Gautama is neither fitting nor is it seemly that the

Sakyas (who were Kshatriyas) menials as they are, mere menials, should neither venerate, nor value, nor esteem, nor give gifts to, nor pay honors to Brahmans."

The Buddha explained to him that these things could not be claimed by a person merely because he was born a Brahman. Such veneration was payable only to a recluse or to a Brahman who had obtained the supreme perfection in wisdom and conduct.

Interestingly enough the Jain Sutras also give instances where Brahmans claimed superiority under their birth alone. This was strongly repudiated by the followers of Mahavira. We have in the Sutrakritanga the following dialogue:

A Vedic Priest: "Those who always feed two thousand holies (Snatak) mendicants, acquire great merit and become Gods. This is the teaching of the Veda".

Ardraka: "He who always feeds two thousand holy cats (i.e. Brahmans), will have to endure great pains in hell, being surrounded by hungry beasts".21

It appears from the above that the Brahmans could not claim any superior position under their birth alone, in eastern India. A Brahman had to earn the position by cultivating the same qualities as an ascetic.

Most of these ascetics practiced severe austerities. Many of them lived completely nude throughout the year. Naturally, some people wondered why these ascetics led such difficult lives. This question occurred to king Ajatashatru of Magadh also. He thought that all persons whether horsemen or charioteers, washer-men or weavers, basket-makers or potters, enjoyed in this very world the visible fruits of their crafts. But was there any such immediate fruit, visible in this very world, of the life of a recluse? When the question first came to the king's mind his ministers advised him to consult some famous recluse who were also heads of their orders and teachers of their schools (of philosophy). The following six religious teachers were named by the ministers of Ajatashatru:

1. Purana Kassapa,
2. Makkhali Goshala,
3. Ajita Keshakamblai,
4. Pakudha kaccayana,
5. Sangyo Belathhiputta, and
6. Ngunit Natapos.

The answers that these teachers gave were not always to the point. They took the opportunity to expound their views on life and human destiny instead of answering the king directly. Another important point to notice is that none of them touched on God, Soul or other intangible subjects. Only one among these six, Sanjaya Belathiputta recognized the possibility of such things, but he was a complete agnostic and his answer to the question of Ajatashatru was: "If you ask me whether there is another world, well, if I thought there were, I would say so. But don't say so. And I don't deny it. And I don't say there neither is nor is not another world. And if you ask me about the beings produced by chance; or whether there is any fruit, any result, of good or bad actions; or whether a man who won the truth continues or not after death to each or any of these questions do I give the same reply."

A teacher who would not answer any question whatsoever would not have many followers. If Sanjaya Belathiputta left behind him any religious group, it did not last long. In fact, in the history of the Indian Philosophy, there have not been many agnostics. But during his lifetime Sanjaya appears to have been quite influential. In the Mahavagga we are told that Sariputta and Mogglayana, the most distinguished pair of the Buddha's disciples had, before their conversion to Buddhism been adherents of Sanjaya and had brought over to the Buddha 250 disciples of their former teacher.

There is, however, an interesting question. Did Sanjay's agnosticism influence the conception of Syadvada or the Satabhangi Nyava of the Jains? Jacobi said in this connection, "Thus, I think, that in opposition to the Agnosticism of Sanjaya, Mahavira has established his Syadvada. For as the

67

Ajnyanavada declares that of a thing beyond our experience the existence or non-existence or simultaneous existence and non-existence, can neither be affirmed nor denied, so in a similar way, but one leading to the contrary results, the Syadvada declares that you can affirm the existence of a thing from one point of view Syadasti, deny it from another Syadasti and affirm both existence and non-existence with reference to it at different times Syad-Asti-nasti. If you should think of affirming existence and non-existence at the same time from the same point of view, you must say that the thing cannot be spoken of Syed vaktavya. Similarly, under certain circumstances, the affirmation of existence is not possible of non-existence Syad nasty avaktavyah and also of both Syad asti nasty avaktavyah.

"This is the famous Saptabhangi Nyaya of the Jains. World and philosopher have enunciated such truisms. The subtle discussion of the Agnostics had probably bewildered and misled many of the contemporaries. Consequently, Syadvada must have appeared to them as a happy way leading out of the adversity of the Ajnyanavada. It was the weapon with which the Agnostics assailed the enemy, turned against them. Who knows how many of their followers went over to Mahavira's creed convinced of the truth of the Saptabhangi Nyaya".

Ajita Kesakambali was a materialist. He used to put on a garment of hair. Hence his name Kesakambali. His answer to Ajatashatru was, "There is no such thing, O king, as alms or sacrifice or offering. There is neither fruit nor result of good or evil deeds. There is no such thing as this world or the next........ Fools and wise alike are cut- off, annihilated, and after death, they are not".

Ajita, of the garment of hair, had a successor called Payasi, who championed Ajita's views. But these people who were usually called Charvakas did not establish any schools. There were, however, individual Charvakas from time to time in all periods of Indian history. They also appear in the epics. For instance, we have a Charvakas called Jabali in the Ramayana. He had accompanied Bharat to request Ram to come back to Ayodhya after Dasaratha's death. As was usual with all Charvakas he was not tactful and said something, which was against conventional wisdom. Jabali had told Ram that it was foolish to suffer the troubles of banishment just to honor the words of a dead father. Again, in the Mahabharata, a Charvakas told Yudhisthira her that he was a sinner for he had killed most of his kinsmen.

Three of the six teachers, viz. Purana Kassapa, Pakudha Kaccayana and Makkhali Gosala gave answers, which were not very dissimilar. Makkhali

Gosala later became the leader of the Ajivika sect. He answered the king Ajatashatru, "There is, O king, no cause either ultimate or remote, for the depravity of being; they become depraved without reason and cause. The attainment of any given condition, of any character, does not depend either on own acts or on the acts of another or human effort. There is no such thing as power or energy or human strength or human vigor........."

It will be seen that the views of Makkhali Gosala, the leader of the Ajivikas, were a sort of determinism (Niyativada). The Ajivikas sect survived for many centuries. Ashok mentions them in one of his pillar edicts. Ashoka's successor Dashrath dedicated a cave in the Barabar hills (in Gaya district) to this sect. The remnants of the Ajivikas were likely absorbed in the Digambaras Jain community. Hoernle in his famous essays on the Ajivikas in Encyclopedia of Religion and Ethics had suggested that one group of the Ajivikas had broken away from Makkhali Gosala when he had abused Mahavira. This breakaway group according to Hoernle had formed the nucleus of the Digambara sect of the Jains.

The answer given by Nigantha Nataputta to King Ajatashatru was "A Nigantha (a man free form bonds), an O king is restrained with fourfold restraint. He lives restrained as regards all water, restrained as regards all evil; all evil has he washed away, and he lives suffused with the sense of evil held at bay. Such is his fourfold self-restraint. And since he is thus tied with this fourfold bond, therefore is he, the Nigantha (free from bonds), called Gatatto (whose heart has gone; that is, to the summit, to the attainment of his aim), Yattatto (whose heart is kept down; that is under command) and Hitatlo (whose heart is fixed).

Nigantha Nataputta has been identified with Mahavira, the Jain Tirthankara. There is, however, little in the above-reported statement of Nigantha Nataputta which can be exclusively related to the Jain principle. The only possible one is the first "restraint" mentioned above viz., the restraint as regard water. This is perhaps the well-known Jain rule not to drink cold water on the ground that there are "souls" in it. There is no doubt that the exact words of Nigantha Nataputta have been greatly distorted as the words passed from one person to another. The Buddhists also would not be too careful to report the beliefs of a rival sect. They might have deliberately distorted the words of the leader of the rival sect. At the same time, it has to be remembered that the Jains claim Ajatashatru as quite friendly towards Mahavira. He would be expected to report faithfully Nataputta words in his talks with the Buddha.

In fact, on closer examination, it will be found that the answers are given by Makkhali Goshala and Nigantha Nataputta, however enigmatic they might appear, bring out the essential philosophic difference between the views of the Ajivikas and the Jains. The Ajivikas deny the existence of free-will, for as Goshala said, "The attainment of any given condition... It does not depend... on any human effort". Nigantha Nataputta, on the other hand, stresses again and again that the restraints Nigantha practices are self- imposed. In other words, the asceticism of a Nigantha is of his own free will.

We thus find that in Magadh in the sixth century BC ., two important things were present in the religious atmosphere. The first is that the most venerated persons in the area were the ascetics. It did not matter to what order or sect the ascetics belonged. All were equally respected. Secondly, the ascetics were not practicing their austerities to gain paradise or any other pleasurable objects. All that they gained in this word was the respect that the people from the king downward paid them.

Asceticism, however, was meant for wholly committed persons. An ordinary man had to take recourse to the worship of Gods and Goddesses for satisfying his religious instinct. The most popular deities in Magadh at that time were the Yakshas. Both Buddhist and Jain canonical works mention the existence of temples of Yakshas both of the male and female species. In fact, according to the ancient Jain works, there were temples dedicated to various Yakshas in every town in northern India. A temple of Bahuputta is mentioned in the Buddhist as well as the Jain texts. This temple had been, according to the Bhagavati-Sutra, the fifth Anga of the Jains, visited by Mahavira himself.

Now, Yakshas were non-Vedic Gods. The term Yakshas, no doubt occurs six times in the Rigveda, but its meaning there is not clear. The Vedic Index 28 says that according to Ludwig it means a feast or a holy practice. The term also occurs several times in the Atharva-Veda. Whitney had translated the term as a monster or prodigy. In any case, the Vedic people never thought of the Yakshas as Gods.

In the later history of Jainism, the Yakshas became attendants of the Tirthankara.

The traditional Jain belief is that Jainism had existed in the same form from the hoary past, and Mahavira the 24th Tirthankara had carried on the religion exactly as it existed in his time, without any change. It would appear from the Jain canonical works themselves, that the traditional answer is not wholly correct. At the time of Mahavira there was indeed an older religion, whose ideals and methods were almost the same as that of Mahavira's and which even his followers called the older section of the Church, but at the same time it is also true that Mahavira did introduce two important changes in the practices of this older section.

The people who are known as Jain's to-day were called Nigganthas in the Swetamber canonical works. Along with the Nigganthas, there was in Magadh another sect who were known as the followers of Parshva. ,The parents of Mahavira were themselves followers of Parshva. The Buddhist describes both the groups as the Niganthas, but the Jain canonical works never say that the Nigganthas and the followers of Parshva were the same people. There were two important differences between the two. The monks among the followers of Parshva could wear clothes, and they had to observe only four vows against the five, which the followers of Mahavira had to observe. At the same time, they were not hostile to each other; they were pursuing, as they said, the same ends. Later, the followers of Parshva joined Mahavira's group. The Uttaradhyayana (23rd lecture) describes how Gautama, the most important disciple of Mahavira's converted Keshi the leader of the followers of Parshva to Mahavira's sect;

1. There was a Jina, Parshva by name, an Arhat worshipped by the people, who was enlightened and omniscient, a prophet of the law and a Jina.

2. And, there was a famous disciple of this Light of the World the young Shaman Keshi, who had completely mastered the sciences and right conduct.

4. Now at that time there lived the Prophet of the Law, the Jina, who in the whole world is known as the venerable Vardhamana.

5. And there was a famous disciple of this Light of the World the venerable Gautama by name that had completely mastered the sciences and right conduct.

6. The pupils of both, who controlled themselves and practiced austerities, who possessed virtues, and protected their self, made the following reflection.

7. Is our Law (i.e., the law of Parshva) the right one, or is the other Law (the Law of Mahavira) the right one? Are our conduct and doctrines right or the other?

8. The Law as taught by the great sage Parshva, which recognizes but four vows or the Law taught by Vardhamana which enjoins five vows?

9. The Law that forbids clothes (for a monk) or that which (allows) an under and an upper garment? Both pursuing the same end, what has caused the difference?

10. Knowing the thoughts of their pupils both Keshi and Gautama made up their minds to meet

each other.

11. Gautama, knowing what is proper and what is due to the older section (of the Church), went to Tinduka Park accompanied by the crowd, his pupils.

The Uttaradhyayana Sutra then describes the long but friendly discussions that took place between Keshi and Gautama. Ultimately Gautama's arguments prevailed and Keshi with his followers accepted Mahavira's teachings. Thus the older section of the Church was absorbed in the section of Mahavira.

Then the Venerable Gautama went with Udaka, the son of Pedhala, to the Venerable Ascetic Mahavira. Then Udaka, the son of Pedhala solemnly circumambulated the Venerable Ascetic Mahavira three times from the left to right, and having done so he praised and worshipped him, and then spoke thus: 'I desire, Reverend Sir, in your presence to passing from the creed which enjoins four vows and the Pratikraman. May it please, beloved of the Gods, do not deny me'

Thus even though the Jain canonical works do not explicitly mention the term

'Niggantha' for them, the followers of Parshva appear to be the older section of the Niggantha Church.

Jacobi, however, puts forward a view that the

followers of Parshva and not the followers of Mahavira were the original Nigantha mentioned by the Buddhists. His argument is as follows:

"In the Majjhima Nikaya 36 (a Pali text), one Shachchaka, the son of a Nigantha explains the meaning of the term Kavya Bhavana, bodily purity, by referring to the conduct of the Achelakas. These Achelakas used to remain stark naked Sabbaso apatichchanna while the Nigantha used some sort of cover. Many of the practices of the Achelakas were identically the same as those observed by the Jains. "And still Sachchaka does not quote the Nigantha as a standard or bodily purity, though he was the son of a Nigantha, and therefore, must have known their religious practices. This curious fact may most easily be accounted for by assuming that the original Niganthas, of whom the Buddhist records usually speak, was not the section of the Church, which submitted to the more rigid rules of Mahavira but those followers of Parshva, who, without forming a hostile party, yet continued to remain within the united Church some particular usage of the old one".

Jacobi's arguments are not very convincing. In any case, it does not explain why, if Mahavira was not a Nigantha according to the Buddhists, their records, continued to call him Nigantha Nataputta till his death. It would appear that so for as the

Buddhists were concerned they called both the sections of the Jain Church, the followers of Parshva, as well as the followers of Mahavira, Niganthas.

We may conclude, therefore, that at the time of the Buddha there existed in Magadh a religious sect known to the Buddhists as the Niganthas. The monks of the older section of this sect observed four vows of asceticism and wore clothes. Mahavira reformed this religion by making two changes: he introduced the fifth vow and forbade the use of clothes by the monks. All the members of the older section accepted these reforms and thereafter there was only one Jain temple.

Eleven

LEGANDARY HISTORY

In the Jain conception, the world has neither beginning in time nor any end. The world and the Jain Church exist eternally. The Jains liken time to a wheel with twelve spokes. The Wheel is going round and round since time began and will go on doing so for all time. At any moment half the wheel is descending. The descending half of the wheel is called Avasarpini, and the ascending half is called Utsarpini. We are living in the Avasarpini half or the descending half of the Time Wheel when human life and manners are becoming worse year by year. Each of these halves is divided into Aras (spokes) or Ages. The Aras in the Avasarpini are the following:

Name of the Age Duration

1. Susama Susama Four crore Sagaropama year

2. Susama Three crore Sagaropama years

3. Susama Dusama Two crore Sagaropama years

4. Dusama susama One crore Sagaropama years less 42,000 ordinary years

5. Dusama 21,000 ordinary years

6. Dusama Dusama 21,000 ordinary years.

Sagaropama or "comparable to the ocean" is a number too large to express in words.

The same Ages occur in the Utsarpini period but the reverse order. In the first Age, in the Susama susama Age, man lived Three palyas or palyopamas a long period not to be expressed in a definite number of years (one crore crone palyas make one "comparable to ocean years). The Nirvana of Rishabha the first Tirthankara occurred 3 years and 8 1/2 months before the end of the third Age. The other 23 Tirthankara was born in the fourth age. Mahavira the last of the Tirthankara died 3 years and 8 1/2 months before the beginning of the fifth age which began in 527 BC We are thus living in the fifth, that is, the Dusama Age. The mythical history of Jainism starts from a period near about the end of the third Age, i.e., the Susama Dusama Age. In this period the first of the sixty-three supermen of the Jain mythology, Rishabhanatha, appeared. The other sixty-two supermen appeared in the fourth, i.e., Dusama-susama Age. The Sve-tambaras call these supermen Shalakapursha, while the Digambaras call them Lakshana-Purusha.1 Mahavira was the last of the sixty-three supermen. Both the Svetambaras and the Digambaras have written many works giving the lives of these sixty-three persons. One of the most famous of these works is the Trishashti shalaka purush- Charitra by Hemachandra. Generally speaking, there is not much difference in the versions of the lives given by the two sects. , The notable differences occur in the case of the two Tirthankara Malli and Mahavira only. In all other cases, the two sects are in agreement about the mythology of their religion.

The sixty-three supermen were the following:

Shvetambara names Digambara names

Tirthankaras Tirthankara 24

Cakravartins Cakravartins 12

Baladeva's Baladevas 09

Vasudevan Narayanan 09

In addition to these sixty-three supermen, there were some kulagaras or legislators. They all arrived in the Third Age. The first Tirthankara Rishabha was also the last of the kulagaras. The kulagaras were the persons who first introduced punishment in the world. These, however, consisted of not more than admonition, warning and reprimands hakkara, Makara and dhikkara.A kulangara was something like Manu, the legislator of the Hindus. Among the Baladevas and Vasudeva's, the most interesting is Balaram and Krishna (Kanha in Prakrit). They appeared at the time of Nemi, the 22nd Tirthankara. Krishna was Nemi's cousin, We get here the Jain version of the Mahabharat The Story of the Kauravas and Pandavas and the descendants of Krishna and Balaram is described. The Kauravas and Pandavas are converted to the Jain religions. Finally, the Pandavas also become ascetics and like Nemi, attain Nirvana.4 One interesting point is that the main battle here is not the one described in the Hindu Mahabharat. Krishna, the Vasudeva, fights a battle with Jarasandha, the Prati Vasudeva, and kills him. This is the main battle in the Jain version. In this battle between Krishna and Jarasandha, the Pandavas take the side of Jarasandha. The main story in this Jain version is the life of Krishna, and this is nearly the same here as given in the Bhagavata Purana of the Hindus. Even otherwise the Krishna is the only Vasudeva who plays some part in the Jain canonical works- Antardasha and Santa Dharma Katha. The Jain version of the Ramayana is given in Padma Caritas or Padma - Puranas. The Padma is the Jain name of Ram and his story in the Jain version differs in many particulars from that of Valmiki. Hemachandra in this Trishashti-shalaka purush- Charitra gives the legend of Ram in detail. According to him, Dasharath, king of Saketa had four queens: Aparajita, Sumitra, Suprabha ad

Kaikeyi. These four queens had four sons. Aparajita son was the Padma, and he became known by the same name as Ram also. Sumitra's son was Narayana: he became to be known by another name, Lakshmana. Kaikeyi's son was Bharata and Suprabha's son was Shatrughna. Sita was the daughter of Janak. She had a twin brother Bhagamandala who was kidnapped while still an infant. Once Janak was attacked by barbarians. Ram was sent to help Janak, and he easily repulsed the enemies. Janak was delighted and wanted Ram to marry his daughter Sita. Dasharath had married Kaikeyi in a svayanvara festival where she had selected him as her husband out of the many kings who had attended the festival. The other kings who were rejected attacked Dasharath. In the battle that ensued, Kaikeyi had acted as the charioteer of Dasharath. She did her job so skillfully that Dashrath had promised her any boon that she desired. She had said that she would ask for her boon on a suitable Occasion. When Dasharath became old he wanted to abdicate and become a beggar. When Kaikeyi heard this she demanded her boon, and this was that her son Bharata should take over the kingdom as Dashrath's successor. Ram readily agreed to this proposal but said that if he stayed on in the capital, Bharata would not accept the throne. He, therefore, thought that he should leave the capital and live in the forest. Sita and Lakshmana accompanied him. The rest of the legend is more or less the same as in Valmiki's Ramayan There is, however, an important difference. It is Lakshmana and not Ram who kills Ravana. In the Jain system, therefore, it is Lakshman who is Vasudeva, Ram

is Baladev, and Ravana is Prati Vasudeva. There is another and perhaps an older version of the Jain Ramayan. This version is given in the 14th Chapter of Sanghadasa'a Vasudeva Hindi and also in the Uttara Purana of Gunabhadra Karya. This version is not popular and is not known to the Svetambaras at all. The story, in brief, is as follows: Dasharath was a king of Varanasi. Ram was his son by his queen Subala, and Lakshman by Kaikeyi. Sita was born to Mandodari, wife of Ravana, but since there was a prophecy that she would be the cause of her father's death, Ravana had sent her through a servant to be buried alive in Mithila. She was accidentally discovered by the king Janak when was plowing the field and brought up as his daughter. When Sita grew up, Janak performed a yajna where Ram and Lakshman were invited. Janak was impressed by Ram's personality and he gave his daughter Sita to him in marriage. Ravana had not been invited to this yajna, and when he heard that Sita was a beautiful girl, he decided to abduct her. There is no mention in this version of the Ramayana of the exile of Rama. Ravana abducts Sita from Citrakuta near Varanasi. Ram recovers her by killing Ravana in Lanka. Therefore Ram and Lakshman come home and rule over their kingdom. All the Chakravarti's have more or less similar careers. Their lives are spent in obtaining the fourteen imperial crown treasures or jewels. After long reigns, they perform the act of purging known as Apurva-karma obtain Keval knowledge and enter Nirvana. The first of the Chakravarti was Bharata, son of the first Tirthankara Rishabha. Rishabh's name occurs in the Hindu Visnu-Purana and Bhagavad Purana also. It is stated there that the emperor Rishabha handed over his empire to his son Bharata and went to the forest where he practiced severe penance and died. He was nude at the time of his death. (This suggests that the Purana story might have come originally from the Jain sources) From the time Rishabha gave away his empire to his son Bharata, they started calling this country Bharata- Varsha. Formerly this country was called Himavarsha. The name of no other Tirthankara is mentioned in the Hindu religious literature. The detailed lives of the twenty-fourth Tirthankara were given in the various Caritas and Puranas has written in the latter part of the first millennium AD the earlier books such as the Kelp

Sutra of the Svetambaras give little details about most of them. The Kalpa Sutra gives some particulars only about the lives of Parshva, Arishtanemi, and Rishabha in a stereotyped manner. It gives the life of Mahavira in some detail, and so far as the other twenty Tirthankara was concerned, mentions only the periods when they appeared. There is some uniformity in the lives of the Tirthankaras. All of them were born of Kshatriya mothers and lived princely lives before they renounced the world, and nearly all of them attained Nirvana in the Sammeta mountain (Parasnath) in Bihar. There were only four exceptions regarding the place of Nirvana. The place of Nirvana of the following four Tirthankaras was as below:

1. Rishabha in Kailasa
12. Vasupujya in Champa
22. Arishtanemi on the Girnar Hills
24. Mahavira in Pava

The twenty-third Tirthankara Parshvanatha is said to have died 250 years before Mahavira, while Parshva predecessor Arishtanemi is said to have died 84,000 years before Mahavira's Nirvana. Naminatha died 5,00,000 years before Arishtanemi and Munisuvrat 1,00,000 years before Naminatha. The intervals go on lengthening until they reach astronomical periods. All the Tirthankaras, except Parshva and Mahavira, are mythical figures. We thus need not discuss their lives given in the various Puranas and Charities. It will, however, be clear from what has been stated above that the Jain's have a philosophy of history (i.e. the theory of the wheel of time) and this is distinct from the philosophy of history of any other people. Also, the Jain's throughout the last fifteen hundred years or so, have taken great delight in writings about the history of their Church up to Mahavira. The Digambaras have practically ignored the history of their church after Mahavira. Except for some pattavalis, which gives the names of their successive Patriarchs, the Digambaras section of the Church has no other history after Mahavira. For Jain sources of the history of the Church after Mahavira, we have therefore to depend on the Svetambaras works only.

Twelve

LIFE OF PARSHAV

Parshva was the twenty-third Tirthankara of the Jains. His historicity is sought to be established by the fact that at the time of Mahavira several people were followers of his teaching. The parents of Mahavira himself were followers of Parshva. In Mahavira's time the leader of this sect, which was called Miganthas by the Buddhists, was Keshi.

The Jain canonical books do not mention much about the life of Parshva. A short account of his life appears in the Kalpa-Sutra of Bhadrabahu. Kalpa Sutra was written perhaps in the 4th or 5th century AD. In the last paragraph of this account, it is mentioned that since the time the Arhat Parshva died twelve centuries have elapsed, and of the thirteenth century that was the thirtieth year. Similarly, in the case of Mahavira, the Kalpa Sutra mentions that since the time of his death nine centuries have elapsed, and of the tenth century that was the eightieth year. From this, we gather that Parshva died 250 years before Mahavira and thus perhaps belonged to the 9th century BC

Apart from this, all the other events in the life of Parshva are written in the stereotyped manner in which the Jains describe the lives of all their Tirthankaras. For instance, it is said that the five most important moments of Parshva's life happened when the moon was in conjunction with the asterism Vishakha. These five events are his conception in the womb of his mother, his birth, his renunciation of the world, his obtaining of supreme knowledge and his death.

Parshva according to the Kalpa Sutra was the son of king Ashwasena of Varanasi. His mother's name was Vama. Parshva lived as a householder for thirty years. He renounced the world at the age of thirty and then practiced severe asceticism for eighty-three days. On the eighty-fourth day, he became a Kevlai, i.e. obtained supreme knowledge. Thereafter he built up a large community of followers both shramnas and householders male as well as female. He died at the age of 100 at Sammeta Sikhara (Parasnath in Bihar).

Thirteen

LIFE OF MAHAVIRA

Vardhamana Mahavira, the twenty-fourth and last
Tirthankaras of the *Jain*s is the most important
figure in the history of Jainism. It was he who con-
solidated the *Jain* Church and laid such a firm foun-
dation for it that it has existed almost unchanged
for more than twenty-five centuries. As already
mentioned, his name, Nigantha Nataputta, occurs
in the early Buddhist records. Since these sources
are independent, they establish the historicity of
Mahavira. The Buddhist records do not give any
details about the life of Mahavira, except to state
that he was a leader of the Nigantha sect. The
Buddhist also records the time of his death. The *Jain*
sources also do not give any particulars about his life
as a teacher. The events before his birth, such as the

90

dreams his mother had when he was conceived are described in great detail, but few details are given about him after he was born. At the age of thirty, Mahavira became an ascetic and wandered about for twelve years. But of Mahavira's life as a teacher for nearly thirty years until his death at the age of 72, the sources are reticent.

The life of Mahavira as we can gather from the Svetambaras sources is as follows:

Mahavira was Kshatriya of the *Jnatri* clan and a native of the (*Kshatriya*) Kundagram, a suburb of the town of Vaishali (near Patna). He was the second son of Siddhartha and Trishala, a highly connected lady. Trishala was the sister of king Chetaka of Vaishali whose daughter Chellana was married to Shrink Bimbisara king of *Magadh*.

The Svetambaras say that the soul of this Tirthankara had first descended into the womb of the Brahman Devananda. Thereafter his fetus had been, by the order of Chakra (Indra) removed thence to the womb of Trishala who gave birth to Mahavira. One may rightly ask how people came to know of this incident of the transfer of the fetus. According to the Svetambaras, it was Mahavira himself who revealed this to his disciples when Devananda once came to see him. This is how it is described in the Bhagavati Sutra.

(The Brahman Rishabh Datta and his wife

Devananda went on pilgrimage to Mahavira). Then milk began to flow from the breast of Brahman woman Devananda, her eyes filled with tears, her arms swelled inside her bangles, her jacket stretched, the hairs of her body stood erect, as when a Kadamba unfolds itself in response to a shower of rain; thus she gazed at the holy monk Mahavira without averting her eyes. "Why master, " said the venerable Gautam to the holy monk Mahavira, "does the Brahman woman gaze…(Thus)…. without averting her eyes?" "Hear, Gautama," Said Mahavira, "The Brahman Woman Devananda is my mother, I am the son of the Brahman woman Devananda. That is why the Brahman woman Devananda gazes at me with tender love, the cause of which is that I first originated in her."

All the five important events in the life of Mahavira, his conception, birth, renunciation of home life, attainment of supreme knowledge, and death occurred when the moon was in conjunction with the asterism Uttaraphalguni. His parents who were pious Jains (i.e. worshippers of Parshva) gave him the name Vardhamana. (Vira or Mahavira is an epithet used as a name). He married Yashoda and by her had a daughter Anojja (also known as Priyadarshana). His parents died when he was 30 years old, and his elder brother Nandivardhana succeeded in his father in whatever position he had held. With the permission of his brother and other authorities, he carried out along cherished resolve and became a monk with the usual Jain rites. Then followed 12 years of

self-mortification. Mahavira wandered about as a mendicant friar bearing all kinds of hardships; after the first 13 months, he even discarded clothes. At the end of this period dedicated to meditation and travels, he reached the state of omniscience (*kevala*) corresponding to the *bodhi* of the Buddhists.

We have some details of Mahavira's itinerary during the twelve years that he roamed about in eastern India before he reached the state of omniscience. Mahavira's life during these twelve years was spent in great difficulties. Sometimes he was taken for a thief by the villagers. Sometimes he and Goshala, his companion for six or seven years were suspected to be spies. The details of his journeys during these twelve years are given in *Jinadasa churni* to the *Avashayaka Sutra*. This *churni* according to Schubring cannot be dated earlier than the 7th century AD, but it is generally taken to be more or less reliable.

Within a few days of Mahavira's renunciation of the world, he went to a village called Kumara. He stood there in meditation for some time. One cow-herder took him to be a thief and wanted to hit him, and Mahavira had to leave the village. Mahavira spent the first rainy season of his ascetic life in Atthiyagama.

During the second year, while Mahavira was crossing the river Suvarnakala, his garment was caught in the thorns on the bank of the river. From this time onwards he remained naked. Mahavira passed his second rainy season in a weaver's shed in Nalanda near Rajagriha. Here Makkhali Gosala met him and became his companion. The two of them left for Kollaga. The third rainy season was passed by Mahavira and Goshala in Champa.

While Mahavira and Goshala were traveling through Coraga Sannivesa they were suspected to be hostile spies and thrown into well. They were however recognized by two female followers of Parshva and were released. They passed the fourth rainy season in Pitthichampa.

The next year of their ascetic lives was very difficult for Goshala and Mahavira. Goshala was apt to mock at people and therefore, was beaten up by them many times. They also traveled to Ladha (south-west Bengal) this year and were ill-treated by the people. They spent the fifth rainy season in Bhaddiya.

In their travels, in this year the two were again taken as spies at a place called Kuvia Sannivesa. They were later released by the intervention of two sisters called Vijaya and Pragalbha. At this time Goshala refused to move in the company of Mahavira, saying that since he was made to bear insults now and then he would prefer to travel alone. They parted company for the time being, but after about six months, when Mahavira was in Salsisygama, Goshala joined him again. They passed the sixth rainy season in Bhaddiya.

They passed their seventh rainy season in Alabhiya. In the next year, Goshala was again beaten-up by the people for his mocking behavior. At one time while the two were in Lohaggala, a place described as the capital of king Jiyasattu, the royal servants took them to be enemy spies and tied them up. Later they were set free by Uppala who is said to have arrived there from Atthiyagama. The eighth rainy season was passed by Mahavira and Goshala in Rayagiha (Rajagriha).

From Rajagriha, Mahavira and Goshala proceeded to Ladha and traveled in Vajjabhumi and Subbhabhumi where Mahavira had to undergo all sorts of torture. These have been described in detail in the Acharanga *Sutra*. An extract is as follows:

"He traveled in the pathless country of the Ladies in Vijjabhumi and Subbhabhumi; he used there, miserable beds and miserable seats. In Ladha (happened) to him many dangers. Many natives attacked him. Even in the faithful part of the rough country the dogs bit him, ran at him. Few people kept off the attacking, biting dogs. Striking the monk, they cried "Chhu Chhu" and made the dogs bite him. Such were the inhabitants. Many other mendicants, eating rough food in Vijjabhumi, and carrying about a strong pole or a stalk(to keep off the dogs), lived there. Even thus armed they were bitten by the dogs, torn by the dogs. It is difficult to travel in Ladha".

They passed the ninth rainy season in this country.

In the tenth year, while the two were in Siddhattha Pura, Goshala finally severed all connections with Mahavira and went to Savatthi. Mahavira then traveled alone for the rest of the year and passed his tenth rainy season in Savatthi.

The exact reason why Mahavira and Goshala parted company is not clear. Perhaps the reason was that Goshala did not care much for chastity and this Mahavira did not like. We have in the *Sutrakritanga* a statement which Goshala, made to Ardraka, a disciple of Mahavira. "As your Law makes it no sin for Mahavira to surround himself by a crowd of disciples, so according to our Law an ascetic, who lives alone and single, does not sin if he uses cold water, eats seeds, accepts things prepared for him, and has intercourse with women."

Goshala spent the last days of his life in Shravasti in the house of a potter woman called Halahala.

It was perhaps after seeing this sort of behavior that Mahavira thought it prudent to make the vow of *Brahmacharya* as one of the necessary conditions of monk-hood and added it to the list of the four vows of Parshva.

The eleventh year of Mahavira was one of his most difficult years. At Tosali he was taken for a robber and hit hard. Then he went to Mosali where he was arrested as a robber but was released by the king's court. When he went back to Tosali the people tried to hang him but he was rescued by a Tosali Kshatriya. The whole of the year was a period of torture and humiliation. He passed his eleventh rainy season in Vesali.

The nest year was of comparative peace. Mahavira passed his twelfth rainy season in Champa.

From Champa, Mahavira reached Jambhiyagama and then journeyed to Mendhiyagama. Then he proceeded to Chammanigama where a cowherd is said to have thrust iron nails into his ears. Mahavira arrived at Majjhima Pava in this condition where the nails were removed from his ears. From here he traveled towards Jambhiyagama, where on the northern bank of the river Ujjuvaliya, in the farm of the householder Samaga, under a Shala tree, in the north-east of Veyavatta shrine, after a period of 12 years 6 months and 15 days, Mahavira attained omniscience (*kevala*) on the bright tenth day of

Vaishakha.

After Mahavira attained Kevala, a *Samavartana* (religious conference) was held on the bank of the river Ujjuvaliya, but it is said that the first preaching of Mahavira remained unsuccessful. Then after traversing twelve *Yojanas*, Mahavira is said to have returned to Majjhima Pava where the second *Samavartana* was convened in the garden of Mahasena. Here, after a long discussion on various religious and philosophic points, Mahavira ordained eleven learned *Brahmins*.

These eleven *Brahman*s later became the eleven *ganaharas* (*Gandhara*) of Mahavira. Nine of them died within the lifetime of Mahavira and only two of them Indabhui Goyama (Indrabhuti Gautam) and Suhamma (Sudharman survived him. Schubring remarks: There can be scarcely any doubt that the other nine *ganadoras* are fictitious."8 In fact, in the *Jain* canonical books, there is scarcely any mention of these nine *ganaharas*.

Mahavira lived for about 30 years after attaining omniscience at the age of forty- two. The *Jain* rules prescribe that during eight months of the summer and winter seasons a monk may stay in a village for one night only and in a town for not more than five nights. During the four months of the rainy season, he should stay in one place. The places where Mahavira spent his forty-two rainy seasons

98

are given in the *Kalpa Sutra*.

The area which Mahavira covered during his ascetic life of 42 years, e.g. from the time he left home and until his death, was roughly Bihar, a part of western and northern Bengal and some parts of eastern Uttar Pradesh. Tosali is also mentioned in some works as a place to which Mahavira went. If this Tosali was in Orissa then Mahavira had gone to that region also.

Most of the early *Jain* works do not take much interest in describing the life of Mahavira after he attained omniscience and became a teacher. There are, however, scattered references here and there. The *Bhagwati Sutra* is the only early work giving comparatively more details of Mahavira's life both before and after he attained omniscience. The later *Jain* writers collected these and other bits of stories about his life and put them in the works called the "Lives of the sixty-three Supermen." Among these works, the most well known is the *Trishashti- Shalaka Purush Charitra* of Hemachandra. Mahavira's life is given in the tenth book of this work. Since Hemachandra was one of the most learned persons among the *Jains*, it may be presumed that he has given in his work, only those parts of the myths and legends connected with Mahavira's life which he found most believable. For Mahavira's life. He had, therefore, filled-up most of his work with the histories of other important people such as the contemporary rulers and their spouses. Sometimes it is difficult to find the relevance of these stories to the life of Mahavira).

Shortly after attaining omniscience Mahavira started wandering in villages, mines, cities, etc., to give help to souls capable of emancipation. Many people would come to see him. Among the first people to him were his natural parents Rishabh Datta and Devananda. It was during this visit that Mahavira recognized Devananda as his mother in whose womb he had first descended from heaven and stayed on for eighty-two days before being transferred to Trishala womb.

Among the early visitors to Mahavira during his wandering were Jamali, his sister's son as well as his son-in-law. Jamali met Mahavira while the latter was in Kshatriya- Kundagram, the village where Mahavira was born. Priyadarshana, Mahavira's daughter, and wife of Jamali had heard a sermon and obtained his parent's consent; he took the vow together with five hundred of the warrior caste. Priyadarshana, Jamali's wife, the Blessed one's daughter, together with one thousand women took initiation under the Master. Then the Blessed one went elsewhere to wander, and Jamali followed him with the warrior-*sadhus*. Over time Jamali, as he wandered, learned the eleven *Angas* and the Lord made him the head of his fellow-mendicants. He practiced penance, two-day fasts, etc. *Priyadarshana* followed Candana.

This Candana was the daughter of Dadhi Vahana, king of Champa. He had been defeated in a battle and his daughter Candana had been enslaved. Once Candana had

given half the food that had been given to her while she was nearly starving to Mahavira as alms. At that time Mahavira had still not attained omniscience. He had taken a vow that he would fast for a long time. It was predicted by the gods, "This girl, who has her last body (before emancipation), averse to the desire for worldly pleasures, will be the first female disciple when Mahavira's omniscience had developed".

One day Jamali bowed to the Lord and said: "With your permission, I and my group shall proceed with unrestricted wanderings." The Blessed One knew by the eye of knowledge that evil would result, and did not answer Jamali asking again and again. With the idea that what is not forbidden is permitted, Jamali and his group separated from the Lord to wander.

While thus wandering along with his followers Jamali once fell ill. He wanted to lie down and asked his men to spread a bed for him. After some time, he asked them whether the bed was spread or not.

They were still spreading the bed and replied that the bed was spread. When Jamali saw that the bed had not until then been spread, he got annoyed with his followers. They replied that according to the teachings of Mahavira "What is being done is done". But now they realized their mistake and knew the truth that "What is being done is not done". This was the sole point in the schism on which Jamali and his group separated from Mahavira. Jamali started boasting that he had attained omniscience. He told Mahavira that he had become all-knowing, all perceiving, an *Arhat* here on earth. His wife Priyadarshana also joined him in his heresy. She, however, realized her mistake by personal experience. Once a person had intentionally allowed a spark of fire to drop on her habit, which caught fire. When she saw that her habit was burning Priyadarshana said, "Look Dhanka, my habit is burnt by your carelessness". Dhanks said, "Do not speak falsely, *Sadhvi*, for according to your doctrine, it is proper to say such a thing when the whole habit has been burnt." Being burnt is burnt' the teaching of Mahavira. "Priyadarshana realized her error in following Jamali's teaching and came back with her followers to her father.

Jamali, however, continued with his false doctrine and at last died without confessing his sin. Jamali's doctrine died with him.

The next important episode described by Hemachandra is the death of Goshala, the leader of the Ajivikas (Hemachandra spells it *Ajivaka*).

In his wanderings, Mahavira had come to Shravasti and stopped there in the garden of one Kosthanka. Goshala had come there earlier and was staying in Shravasti in the shop of a potter woman called Halahala. Goshala used to call himself omniscient. Once while he entered Shravasti for alms, Gautama, one of the chief disciples of Mahavira heard that Goshala was making these claims. Gautama asked Mahavira whether Goshala was right in this matter. Mahavira said: "The son of Mankha, Mankhali, thinking himself a *Jina* though he is not a *Jina*, Goshala is a house of deceit. Initiated by me myself, taught by me, he resorted to wrong belief about me. He is not omniscient, Gautama".

When Goshala heard Mahavira's opinion about him, he was greatly annoyed. When he saw Ananda, another disciple of Mahavira, he threatened that he had a hot flash with which he would consume an enemy. He would destroy Mahavira and his disciples with his flash. When Ananda reported this to Mahavira, he remarked that Goshala indeed had this dangerous flash, with which he could consume anybody except the *Arhat*, who would only feel some discomfort. That is why Goshala should not be teased.

Ananda reported this to the people of Shravasti. This made Goshala angrier, and he came and started abusing Mahavira. Indeed, he was able to kill two of Mahavira's disciples with his hot flash when they tried to remonstrate.

Mahavira tried to pacify Goshala, but Mahavir's words made Goshala angrier, and he discharged his hot flash at Mahavira. "Powerless against the Master like a hurricane against a mountain, it (the flash) circumambulated the Lord, resembling a devotee. From the hot flash, there was only warmth in the Master's body..... The hot flash, as if angry because he had used it for a crime, alas! Turned and entered Goshala body forcibly".

"Burned internally by it, Goshala had recourse to audacity and said arrogantly to the Blessed Mahavira: "Consumed by my hot flash, you will die at the end of six months succumbing to a bilious fever, still an ordinary ascetic, Kashyapa".

"The Master said: "Goshala, your speech is false, since I, omniscient, shall wander for sixteen years more. But you suffering from a bilious fever from your hot flash, will die at the end of the seven days. There is no doubt about it".

"The miserable Goshala, burned by his hot flash drank wine to allay the great heat, accepting a bowl of wine. Intoxicated by the wine he sang and danced and frequently bowed to Halahala (the potter woman), making an *Anjali*….. He spoke disconnected and contradictory speeches, and he passed the day nursed by his sorrowful disciples". Thus he suffered for a week.

At the end of seven days, Goshala repented confessed his errors and died.

(The story of Goshala, taken by Hemachandra mostly from the *Bhagavati-Sutra* probably gives the history of a serious quarrel between the sects of Ajivikas led by Goshala and the Nigganthas led by Mahavira. As described later, Hoernle says in it the signs of the beginning of the *Digambara* Community).

In the course of a few days, Mahavira also became weak from dysentery and bilious fever from the effects of Goshala hot flash, but he did not use any medicine. Rumour spread that he would, as predicted by Goshala, die within six months. His disciples became greatly alarmed and requested Mahavira to take some medicine. At last, Mahavira agreed and said that his disciples should bring that had been cooked by Revati, a housewife, for the household.

"Sinha (one of the disciples) went to Revati's house and got the prescribed remedy

which she gave. Immediately delighted gods made a shower of gold. Lord Vardhamana made use of the excellent medicine brought by Sinha and at once regained health, the full moon to the partridge (*chakra*) of the congregation.

Mahavira lived for sixteen years more after this. He wandered about north Bihar and eastern Uttar Pradesh, teaching people the ethics of his religion. Perhaps nothing very much noteworthy happened during these years.

Mahavira died twenty-nine and half years after he had attained omniscience. The death took place in the house of king Hastipala's scribe in the town of Pava, near Rajagriha. Out of the eleven *Ganadharas*, nine had already died. Only (Indrabhuti) Gautama and Sudharman survived him. A day before his death, Mahavira had sent away Gautama for a day. Perhaps he had feared that Gautama might be too demonstrative of his grief. However, Gautama attained omniscience instantly on the death of Mahavira. He remained in this state for twelve years and on his death Sudharman attained omniscience. Sudharman was the first leader of the *Jain* Church after Mahavira, for Gautama never acted as a teacher.

Svetambaras place the year of the death of Mahavira, which is the initial point of their era, 470 years before the beginning of the Vikram era, or in 527 BC.

On the death of Mahavira, "The light of knowledge having been extinguished, all the kings made material lights. From that time among the people also a festival called Deepotsava, takes place everywhere on that night by making lights".

(Hemachandra in this last part of his *Trishashtishalakapursha- Charitra* has covered nearly all the facts known to the *Jain*s about the life of Mahavira. It is, however, interesting to note that he has not mentioned the second schism of the *Jain* Church. This was started y Tissa Gutta during Mahavira's lifetime, sixteen years after the latter had attained omniscience).

What kind of man was Mahavira? We do not know much about his character from the *Jain* canon, but some conclusions can be drawn from his behavior and sayings. He must have been a man of strong will power and patience. Otherwise, he could have not withstood the tortures and privations he suffered during twelve years he was traveling either alone or with Goshala. His constitution must also have been quite strong.

He was not of a cheerful disposition and disliked mirth among his disciples. We have in the *Acharanga-Sutra*, "A Nirgrantha comprehends (and renounces) mirth, he is not mirthful. The *Kevali*n says: " A Nirgrantha who is moved by mirth, and is mirthful, might utter a falsehood in his speech."

He must have also had charisma and the quality

of attracting people. This conclusion can be drawn from the success he obtained in combining the Nigrantha Church into one and creating a religious system, which has lasted almost unchanged

these 2500 years. His power of attracting people was a cause of envies to his one-time companion and later his rival Makkhali Gosala who complained to Ardraka. "Listen, Ardraka, to what (Mahavira) has done. At first, he wandered about as a single monk; but now he has surrounded himself by many monks, and teaches every one of them the Law at length."

As Jacobi says, "Mahavira must have been a great man in his way, and an eminent leader among his contemporaries; he owed the position of a *Tirthankar* because of the sanctity of his life and his success in the propagating of his creed".

The report about Mahavira's death is also recorded in Buddhist texts. The report appears in three places. These are *Majjhima Nikaya, Samagama Sutta, 3.14; Digha Nikaya, Pasadika Sutta 3.6; and Digha* Nikaya, *Paryaya Sutta* 3.10. The purport of these records is as follows:

Chunda Samanuddesa, a Buddhist monk was passing his rainy season in Pava. At that time the Buddha was dwelling among the Shakkas at Samagama. "Now at that time Nigantha Nataputta had just departed from life at Pava. After his

108

death, the *Niganthas* were divided into two groups. They were making quarrels, making strife, falling into disputes were wounding each other, "You do not know this law of discipline, I know this law of discipline…..You are having false beliefs, I am having true beliefs" etc. Thus the Niganthas of the Nataputta was as if war with each other.

Chunda Samanuddesa after passing the rainy season at Pava went and reported the whole matter to Ananda. Thereupon the venerable Ananda said to him: "Reverend Chunda, this news is worthy to be presented to the Blessed One. Come let us go to the Lord".

Then, the venerable Ananda and Chunda Samanuddesa approached the Buddha, and saluted and sat down at one side and so seated, the venerable Ananda said to the exalted one: "Lord: this Chunda Samanuddesa says "Nigantha Nataputta has just departed…."

This record in the Buddhist text is so vivid, that the obvious inference from it that the Buddha was living at the time of Mahavira's death ought to be accepted. The belief among some scholars, on the other hand, is that it was the Buddha who had died earlier. This latter hypothesis is supported among others by Sinhalese Buddhist tradition that the Buddha died in 544 BC Since the *Jains* believe that Mahavira died in 527 BC, this would put the year of death on the Buddha 16 to 17 years earlier than the year of Mahavira's death. Things are, however, not free from complications. Hemchandra, the historian of the *Jain* Church, has written that Chandragupta Maurya became emperor 155 years after the death of Mahavira. This would bring the years of the death of Mahavira to 468 BC There are other traditions also about the years of the death of Mahavira and the Buddha.

Fourteen

THE JAIN CHURCH AFTER MAHAVIRA

The last part of Bhadreshwar Kathavali, a huge work in Prakrit prose. Both these are legendary histories or rather hagiographies, i.e. they give mostly the legends connected with the lives of these patriarchs and the contemporary kings. The "history" of the Jain Church as given below is mostly based on Hemachandra's Sthaviravada. A large part of the Sthaviravada describes the good deeds done by the patriarchies in their previous births as a result of which they were rewarded with saintly lives in their present births. The work also describes the political events of the period, especially about the influence that the Jain had on these events. These descriptions are of general interest. (The events are perhaps

111

described as the Jains would like them to have happened, and not necessarily as they happened).

"Sudharman entered the order at the age of fifty; thirty years he was the disciple of Mahavira, twelve years after whose death he reached kevalam. He died eight years later, having accomplished his 100th year". "Sudharman's successor was Jambu. It is related that once Sudharman, surrounded by his disciples, Jambu, etc., arrived in Champa, and took up his abode in the part outside the town. As was usual, a crowd gathered to hear his preaching. King Kunika (Ajatashatru) saw the crowd and came to hear the sermon. When the sermon was at an end, the king asked Sudharman who Jambu was, for the king greatly struck with the beauty and the remarkable appearance of Jambu. Sudharman related to him Jambu's history and foretold that he would be the last kevalin. After him nobody would reach Manahpayaya and the Paramvadhi stages of supernatural knowledge; the JinaKalpa would be abandoned together with other holy institutions and practices, while on earth the sanctity of men would go on decreasing".

Here perhaps we get the first hint of the schism between the Shvetambara and the Digambara Churches. One of the practices of Jina Kalpa is the complete nudity of the monks. The Svetambara monks have abandoned this practice and follow

112

what is known as sthavir-Kalpa. It is interesting to note that the name of Jambu's successor Prabhava who presumably followed the sthavira Kalpa does not appear in any of the lists of patriarchs of the Digambaras.

"Jambu reached beatification 64 years after Mahavira's Nirvana, having appointed Prabhava of the Katyayana gotra as the visible head of the Church".

Shayyambhava was born a heretic and at first, he studied the Vedic religion under his guru. Once he met two monks who said: "Ah, you know not the truth." This unsettled his mind and a few days later he took farewell of his guru and went in search of the two monks. At lasts, he came to Prabhava from whom he asked for instruction in the Jain religion. Prabhava explained to him the five vows of the Jains; and when Shayyambhava had renounced his former heretical views, he received Diksha and became a zealous ascetic. He learned the fourteen Purvas and became, after Prabhava's death, the head of the Church".

When Shambhava took Diksha, he had left his young wife behind. They had as yet no children. The circumstances made the forsaken woman's case appear still more miserable so that people compassionately asked her if there was no hope of offspring. She answered in Prakrit, "manayam" i.e. "a little". Hence the boy to whom she eventually

113

gave birth, was called Manaka. When Manaka was eight years old and became aware that his mother was not dressed like a widow, he asked her who his father was. He then learned that his father was Shayyambhava, who, becoming a monk, had left before he, Manaka, was born, and never returned. Manka who yearned for his father secretly left his mother and went to Champa. There he met his father, and as he did not recognize him as such, he inquired of him about his father by whom he wanted to be ordained. Upon which Shayyambhava gave himself out as the most intimate friend of his father in whose stead he would ordain him. Manaka agreeing to this Shayyambhava brought him to the monks without explaining the relation subsisting between the boy and himself. The boy was ordained. Shayyambhava through his supernatural knowledge perceived that his son would die in six months. The time is too short for mastering the whole sacred lore, in extensor, Shayyambhava condensed its essence in ten lectures, which he composed in the afternoon. Hence the work is called Dashavaikalika. For thought to make abstracts of the Law is allowed to none but the last Dashapurvin, yet under certain circumstances, a Shrutakevalin may do so. Manaka learned the Dashavaikalika, and thus he was well instructed in the religion. When the six months were over and he died, Shayyambhava wept so much

114

at Manaka's death that his disciples were at a loss to comprehend his deportment which appeared so unbecoming of a world-renouncing monk, and said as much. He then told them Manaka's history and declared that he wept for joy because his son had died a saint. The disciples learning then that Manaka was their acharya's son wondered why he had not told them this before. Shayyambhava replied that if they had known Manaka to be his son, they would not have exacted the obedience, which is the duty of every novice, and the most meritorious part of his moral exercise. He added that for the sake of Manaka's instruction, he had composed Dashavaikalika, but now the object is attained, he would cause his work to disappear. The disciples, however, moved the Sangha to solicit Shayyambhava that he should publish the Sashavaikalika. Shayyambhava complying with their wishes, that work has been preserved." At last Shayyambhava died, having appointed Yash Bhadra as his successor". "After a most exemplary life of an ascetic and a teacher, Yashodhara died leaving the management of the Church to his disciples Bhadrabahu and Sambhutavijaya".

Hemchandra in his Sthaviravada now goes back about a hundred years to the time when Pataliputra, the new capital of Magadh, was founded. Later he describes the political history of the period of

115

Nandas and the Mauryas and then comes back to the history of the Jain Church.

"Kunika was the king of Magadh at the time of Mahavira. Kunika's capital was Champa. When he died, his son Udayin succeeded him. Everything in his residency brought back to him the memory of his deceased father and rendered him exceedingly sad. His Ministers, therefore, persuaded him to found a new capital, just as Kunika had founded Champa, after leaving Rajagriha on the death of his father. To find a site suitable for the future capital, Udayin dispatched men versed in the interpretation of omens. When they had reached the bank of the Ganga, they came upon a magnificent Patali tree. On a bough of this tree was perched a Chasa bird. The bird opened from time to time its bill in which insects fell by themselves. The augurs noticing this remarkable omen returned to the King and recommended the spot for erecting the new Capital. An old auger then declared that the Patali tree was not common, for he had heard from wise men a story about it. The story was about one Annika Putra who had even in a painful situation succeeded in concentrating his thoughts, and thus, at last, reached Nirvana, which event was duly celebrated by the gods near this place. This place henceforth became a famous tirtha called Prayaga. The skull of Annika Putra was drifted down by the river and landed on the bank. There the seed of a Patali tree found its way into it, and springing up it developed into the tree that was to mark the site of the new capital. In the center of this city, a fine Jain Temple was raised by the order of the monarch who was a devout Jain.

How Nanda became king of Magadh?

"Udayin the king of Magadh was murdered by the agent of a rival king. Udayin was childless. His ministers, therefore, sent the Royal Elephant in a procession through the main street for searching out the next king. At that moment Nanda was coming from the opposite side in his marriage procession. Nanda was the son of the courtesan by a barber. When the two processions met, the State Elephant put Nanda on his back, the horse neighed, and other such auspicious omens were seen. In short, it was evident that the royal insignia themselves pointed him out as the successor of Udayin. He was accordingly proclaimed king and ascended the throne. This event happened sixty years after the Nirvana. The name of Nanda's minister was Kalpaka.

Sthulabhadra

Seven descendants of Nanda succeeded each other. The ministers of these Nanda monarchs were the descendants of Kalpaka. The minister of the ninth Nanda was also a descendant of Kalpaka. His name was Sakatala. Sakata La had two sons, Sthulibhadra and Shriyaka. Shriyaka was in the service of the king whose confidence and love he had gained.

On the death of Sakatala, the king offered Shriyanka the seal of the Prime Minister, but he refused it in favor of his brother Sthulibhadra. Accordingly, the same offer was made to Sthulibhadra, who said that he would consider the matter. Ordered to make up his mind without delay, his reflections took an unexpected turn; for perceiving the vanity of the world he resolved to quit empty pleasures, and plucking out his hair he acquainted the king with his resolution. He later took Diksha under Sambhuta Vijaya.

Chanakya and Chandragupta

Chanakya was the son of the Brahman Chanin, a devout Jain. Once Chanakya was thrown out of the court of the ninth Nanda. It was Chanakya's fault, for he had behaved quite impertinently, but he was very sore at the insult and wanted his revenge. He met Chandragupta and induced him to attack Pataliputra, the capital of the Nandas. But every time Chandra Gupta did this he was defeated. Chanakya then adopted the policy of subduing the outlying districts first. One of these towns was defending itself very resolutely. Chanakya learned that the town was protected by the idol. Chandragupta then conquered the town. One by one Chandragupta captured all the outlying towns and was able finally to take Pataliputra, where he ascended the throne. This event happened 155 years after Mahavira's Nirvana. Chandra Gupta chooses Jain teacher s at Chanakya's instance

In the beginning, Chandragupta preferred heretic teachers. To prove that heretic teacher were worthless, Chanakya once invited them to the palace. He placed some dust on the floor near the window overlooking the royal seraglio. When no palace servant was there, the heretic teachers went and looked through the window. Chanakya showed their footprints to the king, and thus proved that these heretic teachers were looking at women. The Jain teachers, however, who were invited the next day, remained in their seats from the beginning till the end of their visit, and this time, of course, the dust on the floor in front of the windows was found untouched. Chandragupta seeing the proof of the sanctity of the Jain teachers henceforth made them his spiritual guides.

Birth of Bindusara and death of Chandragupta

Chanakya served Chandragupta as his minister throughout the life of later. "On Chanakya's order, the food of Chandragupta was mixed with a gradually increased dose of poison, so that in the end even the strongest poison did not affect him. Once the queen Durdhara who was big with the child was dining with the king when Chanakya came upon them. Observing that the poison almost instantly killed the queen he ripped open her womb and extracted the child. He had been near too late; for already a drop of the poison had reached the boy's head, who, from these circumstances was called Bindusara. In ripe age, he was placed on the throne by Chanakya on the decease of his father who died by samadhi."

Ashoka and Samprati

"On Bindusara's decease, his son Ashoka Shri ascended the throne. Ashoka sent his son and presumptive heir, Kunala, to Ujjayini, there to be brought up. When the prince was eight years old, the king wrote (in Prakrit) to the tutors that Kunala should begin his studies. One of Ashoka's wives who wanted to secure the succession to her son being then present took up the letter to read it, and secretly putting a dot over the letter 'a', changed Adheeyu into Andheeyu another word, meaning he must be blinded. Without rereading the letter, the king sealed and dispatched it. The clerk in Ujjayini was so shocked by the contents of this letter that he was unable to read it aloud to the prince. Kunala, therefore, seized the letter and read the cruel sentence of his father. Considering that as yet no Maurya prince had disobeyed the chief of the house, and unwilling to set a bad example, he stoutly put out his eyesight with a hot iron".

"Years later Kunala came to Ashoka's court dressed as a minstrel and when he greatly pleased the king by his music, the king wanted to reward him. At this, the minstrel was Prince Kunala and he was demanding his inheritance. Ashoka sadly objected that being blind Kunala never could ascend the throne. Thereupon the latter said that he claimed the kingdom not for himself but his son. "When", cried the king, "has a son been born to you?" "Just now Samprati) was the answer. Samprati accordingly was the name given to Kunala son, and though a baby in arms, he was anointed Ashoka's successor, after whose demise he ascended the throne and became a powerful monarch. Samprati was a staunch Jain".

121

Hemachandra then describes how the ten Purvas were preserved by Sthulibhadra. The principal character in this famous incident was Bhadrabahu, and Bhadrabahu died 170 years after the Nirvana of Mahavira, i.e. fifteen years after the accession of Chandragupta, it is clear that the incident described below happened during the reign of Chandragupta.

Sthula Bhadra learns the Purvas from Bhadrabahu.

"A dreadful dearth prevailing about this time forced the monks to emigrate as far as the seaside. During these unsettled times, they neglected their regular studies so that the sacred lore was on the point of falling into oblivion. The Sangha, therefore, reassembling at Pataliputra when the famine was over, collected the fragments of the canon which the monks happened to recollect, and in this way brought together eleven Angas. To recover the Drishtivada, the Sangha sent monks to Bhadrabahu in Nepal commanding him to join the Council. Bhadrabahu, however, declined to come, as he had undertaken the Mahaprana vow, which it would take 12 years to carry out; but after that period he would in a short time teach the whole of the Drishtivada. Upon receiving the answer, the Sangha again dispatched two monks to ask Bhadrabahu what penalty he who disobeyed the Sangha incurred. If he should answer excommunication, then they should reply that such was his punishment. Everything coming about as foreseen, Bhadrabahu requested some clever monks to whom he would daily deliver seven lessons at a suitable time. Accordingly, 500 monks with Sthulabhadra as their leader, were sent to Bhadrabahu. But all of them except Sthulibhadra, becoming tired by the slowness of their progress, soon fell off; Sthulibhadra alone stayed out the whole term of his master's vow. At the end of it, he had learned the first ten Purvas.

Sthulabhadra and Bhadrabahu, it appears, then went back to Pataliputra. Sthulibhadra had seven sisters. These sisters of Sthulibhadra paying their reverence to Bhadrabahu after his arrival in Pataliputra asked him where their brother stayed, and were directed to some temple. On their approach, Sthulibhadra transferred himself into a lion, to gratify his sisters with the sight of a miracle. Of course, the frightened girls ran back to their guru to tell him that a lion had devoured their brother. Bhadrabahu, however, assured them that their brother was alive, and so they found him on their return to the temple".

"When his sisters had left Sthulibhadra, he went to Bhadrabahu for his daily lesson. But the latter refused to teach him any more, as he had become unworthy of it. Sthulibhadra then replied that he remembered no sin since his ordination, but being reminded by him of what he had done, he fell at his feet and implored his forgiveness. Bhadrabahu, however, would not take up his instruction. Even the whole Sangha could only with great difficulty overcome his reluctance. He, at last, consented to teach Sthulibhadra the rest of the Purvas on the condition only that they (viz. He should not hand down the last four Purvas) to anybody else. On Bhadrabahu's death, 170 years after Mahavira's Nirvana, Sthulibhadra became the head of the Church.)

Mahagiri & Suhastin

"Sthulibhadra had two disciples, Mahagiri and Suhastin. As Yaksarya brought them up, the word Arya was prefixed to their names. Sthulibhadra taught them the ten Purvas, for the last four Purvas he was forbidden to teach. After their teacher's decease, they succeeded in his place."

"After some time, Mahagiri made over his disciples to Suhastin and lived as aJinakalpika, though the Jina Kalpa had by that time fallen into disuse."

Hemchandra had stated earlier that Jina Kalpa was abandoned after Jambu. Does Mahagiri's acceptance of Jeena Kalpa signify the break up of the Jain Church into the two sects Digambara and Svetambara? This does not appear to be the case, for Mahagiri's name does not figure in any list of sthaviras of the Digambaras. Also, Hemachandra's statement that Mahagiri had handed over his disciples to Suhastin is perhaps not correct for Nandi Sutra, a Svetambara text gives the succession list of Mahagiri's disciples, and this list is completely different from the list of successors of Suhastin given in the Kalpa Sutra.

In other words, when Mahagiri started living as a Jina Kalpa, he either had not made over his disciples to Suhastin or if he had done so, then he might have had picked up a new group of disciples later. One thing is clear: Mahagiri's successors did not leave many impresses on the history of Jainism. Except for the Nandi Sutra list, their names have practically disappeared. As stated earlier the only one whose name occurs in the legends composed in the latter times was Mangu.

Spread of Jainism

Buddhism had spread all over India and to some places outside India due to the missionary efforts of Ashoka. A similar role in the case of Jainism was played, according to Hemachandra, by Ashoka's grandson Samprati. Hemachandra continues.

"The king (Samprati) looking up to Suhastin as his greatest benefactor, was converted by him to the true faith, and henceforth strictly performed all duties enjoined to the laity. He further showed his zeal by causing Jina Temples to be erected over the whole of Jambudvipa".

"The example and advice of Samprati induced his vassals to embrace and patronize his creed so that not only in his kingdom but also in the adjacent countries, the monks could practice their religion."

"To extend the sphere of their activity to uncivilized countries, Samprati sent their messengers disguised as Jain monks. They described to the people the kind of good and other requisites which monks accept as alms, enjoining them to give such things instead of the usual taxes to the revenue collectors who would visit them from time to time. Of course, these revenue collectors were to be Jain monks. Having thus prepared the way for them, he induced the Superior to send monks to these countries, for they would find it in no way impossible to live there. Accordingly, missionaries were sent to the Andras and Dramilas, who found everything as the king had told. Thus the uncivilized nations were brought under the influence of Jainism".

"Such was the religious zeal of the king (Samprati) that he ordered the merchants to give the monks gratis all things they should ask for and to draw on the royal treasury for the value of the goods. It may be imagined that the merchants did not hesitate to obey the king's order".

"Although the alms with which the monks were supplied are expressly forbidden by the rules of the Church, Suhastin, afraid to offend the zealous king, dared not make any opposition. Mahagiri, therefore, severely blamed Suhastin, and resolved definitely to separate from him. For as he said, there was an old prophecy that after Sthulibhadra, the conduct of the Jains would deteriorate. Accordingly, after saluting the image of Jivantasvamin, he left Avanti and went to the Tirtha Gajendra Panda. There, starving himself to death, he reached Svarga. Samprati dying at the end of his reign, during which he continued a patron of the Jains, became a God and at last, he will reach Siddhi".

The Temple of Mahakal in Ujjain

There was a merchant's son called Avantis Vimala. Once he heard the preaching of Suhastin and was thus greatly attracted to Jainism. He became a monk, but as he was of a delicate constitution, he could not stand the rigor and died while starving. His son built a magnificent temple at the spot where his father so manfully had faced death. This temple is still famous in the world as the temple of Mahakala.

(Hemachandra does not say so specifically, but the implication clearly is that this temple was originally a Jain temple, and was later converted into a Hindu temple by the Shaivites. In the thirteenth century (AD 1234) Iltutmish destroyed this temple. Ramchandra, Diwan of the Peshwa built the present temple of Mahakala on the same site, in 1745.)

"Over time, Suhastin left this world starving himself to death, and entered heaven". Hemachandra then leaves out the next four patriarchs from Suhastin onwards are as follows: 8 Suhastin. 9 Susthira- Supratibuddha. 10 Indra. 11 Dinna. 12 Sinhagiri. 13 Vajra.

Hemachandra does not mention Sustaita, Indra, and Dinna at all, and mentions Sinhagiri only as of the guru of Vajra.

Vajra was the son of Dhanagiri, a disciple of Sinhagiri. Dhaulagiri had left his house soon after his wife became pregnant. The child who was born to this abandoned woman was very troublesome and her relations gave him away to Sinhagiri when he had come to the area on a preaching mission. Since the child was very heavy in weight Sinhagiri named him Vajra. He was then educated in the sacred literature. Sinhagiri wanted Vajra to be master in the knowledge of the sacred books, so he sent Vajra to Bhadra Gupta in Ujjain. Bhandragupta was a master of ten Purvas.

"Soon afterward Vajra arrived and was most cordially received by Bhandragupta, who readily imparted to him the knowledge of the Purvas. The object of Vajra's mission being accomplished in a short time, he returned to Dashapura and joined his guru. The latter permitted him to teach the Purvas, which event the Gods celebrated by showering down a rain of flowers. Sinhagiri, after having made over to Vajra, his gana, put an end to his earthly career by self- starvation. Vajurasvamin, then traveling about in company with 500 monks preached the Law; wherever he went he was admired and praised by all."

How the knowledge of the latter part of the 10th Purva was lost?

There was a person called Arya Rakshita. He went to great acharya to learn the Drishti Vada. The Acharya asked him to become a monk first. Arya Rakshita was willing to do so at once, but he induced the monks to remove their residence; for he was afraid that the king and the people would importune him to leave the order. (This was the first case that Jains were guilty of seducing disciples of other sects.) Arya Rakshita became a pious monk and he readily acquired all knowledge that the acharya possessed. But when he was told that Vajra in Puri knew more of the Drishti Vada than his teacher, he went and joined Vajra.

Then Arya Rakshita began his studies and in a short time had mastered nine Purvas. It was when he learned the yamakas of the 10th Purva that the course of his studies was interrupted. For about this time a letter arrived from his parents entreating him to return home. Vajra was at first reluctant to let him go without learning all the Purvas, but when more such letters came requesting Aryaraksita to go back home, "Vajra at last permitted him to go, because his intuition told him that he (Vajra) should soon die, and with him the knowledge of the complete 10th Purva." (XIII, 134) "With Vajra died out the knowledge of the complete 10th Purva, and the fourth Samhanana came to its end."

"From Vajra are derived all the divisions of the Church which exist at present."Thus Hemachandra ends the Sthaviravada, the history of the patriarchs of the Jain Church. In the 13th canto of his work, he mentions one or two incidents from the life of Vajrasana who was the successor of Vajra, but these are not important in the history of the Church. (Arya Rakshita whom Vajra had taught most of the Purvas never became a patriarch, but his pupil Gotta

Mahila was the person who started the seventh schism of the Jain Church in 584 AV.).

It appears from the account given by Hemachandra that generally, it was one person who occupied the top place in the Church, and this person was the one who knew the Jain sacred literature in full. There was up to that time no written record of this literature and everything had to be committed to memory. People with such good memory are not easy to find at any time, and the Jains had to find such men among the limited number of people who would accept the strict rules of the Jain monk-hood. Only twice there were two heads of the Church living simultaneously. The second of this occasion was during the reign of king Samprati in Ujjain. At that time Mahagiri and Suhanstin headed the Church simultaneously. Of the two, Mahagiri was conservative. He wanted the Jain monks to live strictly in the manner prescribed in the Law. Since he was unable to enforce this, he went away and starved himself to death.

The headquarters of the Jain Church was generally in the capital city of the most powerful ruler of that time. When Udayin, founded his new capital city at Pataliputra, the headquarters of the Church was moved there. It remained there throughout the Nandas and the first three Mauryas. When the fourth Maurya king Samprati (one of

Ashoka's grandsons) set up his capital to Ujjain, the headquarters of the Jain Church also moved there.

As noted earlier Hemachandra does not describe the lives of the four patriarchs between Suhastin and Vajra. These four patriarchs are named in the Kalpa Sutra. A question may be raised as to whether even this Kalpa Sutra list is a complete one, for the possibility is that the number of patriarchs between Suhastin and Vjra was more than four. Jacobi arrives at this conjecture on the following basis;

Hemachandra mentions that Bhadrabahu died 170 years (170 AV.) after the Nirvana of Mahavira. As Bhadrabahu was the sixth patriarch, this gives an average period of a little less than thirty years for each patriarch up to Bhadrabahu.

On the other hand, if we accept the usual date given for the sixth schism to be 544 AV., then we find the difference between the lifetime of its author Rohagutta and the death of Bhadrabahu as 374 years. Now, Rohagutta8 was a prashishya of Suhastin, the eighth patriarch, e.g., he belonged to the generation of the tenth patriarch. This gives only four patriarchs in 374 years that means 94 years for each patriarch. This according to Jacobi is an absurd figure. It may be questioned whether the date of the sixth schism, viz. 544 AV. is correctly recorded. Jacobi has also examined this point. The first seven schisms of the Jain Church have been described in the Avashyakta Nirukti, but it does not mention the eighth schism (the Svetambara-Digambara split) which is said to have taken place in 609 AV.), or, say, 50 to 60 years after the 6th schism (544 AV.). So there is not much possibility that the date of this schism could have been forgotten by that time. "To sum up, if we base our inquiry on the well-established date of the schisms,9 we conclude that the list of Theras (patriarchs) is imperfectly handed down; there must have been far more theras than are contained in the Theravalis."

"In other words, the Theravalis do not furnish a connected list of patriarchs succeeding each other as teacher and disciple, but a patched up list of patriarchs whose memory survived in oral and literary tradition, while the rest of them had fallen in utter oblivion."

It will be noticed that Hemachandra ends his *Sthaviravada* in an enigmatic manner. "From Vajra are derived all the divisions of the Church which exist at present." What these divisions were, are not stated. It may be conjectured that Vajra had supported *chaityavasa* (dwelling by monks in temples a practice that led later to corruption among the *Svetambaras*. An inscription of about the 1st century AD on the Son Bhandara (Rajgir, Bihar) shows that *Acharya* Vaira (Vajra) excavated two caves that were suitable for dwellings of monks and in which *Jain* images were installed for worship.

Fifteen

JAIN LITERATURE

Canonical and commentarial literature.

Jain canonical scriptures do not belong to a single period, nor is any text free from later revision or additions. The sacred literature, transmitted orally, was first systematized in a council at Patna about the end of the 4th century BCE, of which little can be said, and again in two later councils at Mathura (early 3rd century CE) and Valabhi. The fourth and last council, at Valabhi in the mid-5th century, is considered the source of the existing Shvetambara canon, though some commentators insist that the present version comes from the Mathura council.

The original, unadulterated teachings of the

Tirthankaras, the Purvas, are said to have been contained in 14 ancient or "prior" (*Purva*) texts, which are now lost. Svetambaras and Digambaras agree that a time will come when the teachings of the Tirthankaras will be completely lost; Jainism will then disappear from the earth and reappear at an appropriate point in the next time cycle (*Kalpa*). The two sects disagree, however, about the extent to which the corruption and loss of the Tirthankaras' teachings have already occurred. Consequently, the texts for each sect differ.

The Svetambaras embrace an extensive *agama* (Sanskrit: "tradition," or "received teachings"; i.e., collection of canonical texts) as the repository of their tradition. Based upon what are believed to be discourses by Mahavira that were compiled by his disciples, this canon imperfectly preserves his teachings, since it has been subject to both interpolation and loss throughout the ages. The number of texts considered to make up the Shvetambara canon has varied over time and by the monastic group. Largely through the influence of the 19th-century Austrian scholar Johann Georg Bühler, however, Western scholars have fixed the number of texts in this canon at 45, divided into six groups: the 11 *Anga*s ("Parts"; originally there were 12, but one, the *Drishti Vada*, has been lost), 12 *Upanga*s (subsidiary texts), 4 *Mula-sutra*s (basic texts), 6 *Cheda-sutra*s (concerned with discipline), 2 *Chulika-sutras* (appendix texts), and 10 *Prakirnakas* (mixed, assorted texts). The *Angas* contain several dialogues, mainly between Mahavira and his disciple Indrabhuti Gautama, presumably recorded by the disciple Sudharman, who transmitted the teachings to his disciples.

According to modern scholars, the *Acharanga* (first chapter) and the *Sutrakritanga*, among the *Angas*, and sections of the *Uttaradhyayana*, among the *Mula-sutras*, represent the oldest parts of the canon. The fifth *Anga*, the *Bhagavati*, is an extensive repository of early Jain teachings. The *Cheda-sutra text Dashashrutaskandha* concludes with the ritually important *Kalpa-sutra*, which recounts the lives of the Jinas and includes an appendix of rules for monastic life and a list of eminent monks.

Bhadrabahu, traditionally recognized as the last Jain sage to know the contents of the *Purvas*, is thought to be the author of the *Niryuktis*, the earliest commentaries on the Jain canonical texts. These concise, metrical commentaries, written in Prakrit, gave rise to an expanded corpus of texts called *Bhashyas* and *Churnis*. Composed between the 4th and the 7th century, these texts contain many ancient Jain legends and historical traditions and a large number of popular stories that support Jain doctrine. The *Bhashyas* and *Churnis*, in turn, gave rise in the medieval period to a large collection of Sanskrit commentaries. Haribhadra, Shilanka, Abhayadev, and Malayagiri are the best-known authors of such commentaries.

Digambaras give canonical status to two works in Prakrit: the *Karmaprabhrita* ("Chapters on Karma"), also called *Shatkhandagama* ("Scripture of Six Sections"), and the *Kashayaprabhrita* ("Chapters on the *Kashayas*"). The *Karmaprabhrita*, allegedly based on the lost *Drishti Vada* text, deals with the doctrine of karma and was redacted by Pushpadanta and Bhutabalin in the mid-2nd century; the *Kashayaprabhrita*, compiled by Gunadhara from the same source about the same time, deals with the passions (*kashaya*) that defile and bind the soul. Later commentaries by Virasena (in the 8th century) and his disciple Jinasena (in the 9th century) on the *Kashayaprabhrita* are also highly respected by Digambaras.

The religious merit that accrues from hearing and reading Jain texts encouraged the careful and loving preservation of manuscripts. The Jains have traditionally maintained important libraries throughout India, among the most significant of which are those for the Svetambaras at Chambay (or Khambhat), Patan (both in Gujarat state), and Jaisalmer (Rajasthan) and those for the Digambaras at Karanja (Maharashtra) and Mudbidri (Karnataka). The miniatures on palm-leaf and paper manuscripts and wooden book cover preserved in the Jain monastic libraries provide a continuous history of the art of painting in western India from the 11th century to the present.

Philosophical and other literature

In addition to their canons and commentaries, the Svetambara and Digambara traditions have produced a voluminous body of literature, written in several languages, in the areas of philosophy, poetry, drama, grammar, music, mathematics, medicine, astronomy, astrology, and architecture. In Tamil the epics *Chilappathikaram* and *Jivaka Chintamani*, which are written from a Jain perspective, are important works of early post-classical Tamil literature. Jain authors were also an important formative influence on Kannada literature. The Jain lay poet Pampa *Adipurana*(another text dealing with the lives of Rishabha, Bahubali, and Bharata) is the earliest extant piece of *maha kavya* ("high poetic") Kannada literature. Jains were similarly influential in the Prakrit languages, Apabhramsha, Old Gujarati, and, later, Sanskrit. A particular forte of Jain writers was narrative, through which they promoted the religion's ideals. The most remarkable example of this is the huge Sanskrit novel *The Story of Upamiti's Series of Existences* by the 10th-century Shvetambara monk Siddharshi.

Of particular importance, both as a systemization of the early Jain worldview and as an authoritative basis of later philosophical commentary is the *Tattvartha-sutra* of Umasvati, whose work is claimed by both the Digambara and Umasvamin communities. Composed early in the Common Era, the *Tattvartha-sutra* was the first Jain philosophical work in Sanskrit to address logic, epistemology, ontology, ethics, cosmography, and cosmogony.

Digambaras also value the Prakrit works of Kundakunda (*c.* 2nd century, though perhaps later), including the *Pravachanasara*(on ethics), the *Samayasara* (on the essence of doctrine), the *Niyamasara* (on Jain monastic discipline), and the six *Prabhrita*s ("Chapters"; on various religious topics). Kundakunda's writings are distinguished by their deployment of a two-perspective (*Naya*) model, according to which all outward aspects of Jain practice are subordinated to an inner, spiritual interpretation.

The details of Jain doctrine did not change much throughout history, and no major philosophical disagreements exercised Jain intellectuals. The main concerns of the medieval period were to ensure that scriptural statements were compatible with logic and to controvert the rival claims of the Hindus and the Buddhists.

140

Sixteen

THE SCHISMS

The Main schism of the Jain Church was the one between the Svetambaras and the Digambaras. The Svetambaras believe that even before this schism, there had been seven other schisms. These schisms had started when certain important leaders of the Church had disagreed with the views of the Main Church on some points of philosophy or ritual. These leaders had then taken away their followers and established what one might call separate sects. However, these schisms had little permanent effects, for the newly formed sects had either disappeared or had joined the main Church again on the death of their leaders. The seven schisms have been all described together in Avashyak Niryukti(The Digambaras do not know of these seven schisms at

142

all.)

The first of these schisms, as we have already seen, happened during the life of Mahavira himself. Its leader was his son-in-law Jamali. Jamali broke away with his followers from Mahavira fourteen years after the latter had attained omniscience. The point on which Jamali differed from Mahavira would appear to an outsider to be a mere quibble.

The second schism was started by Tissagutta in Rajagriha. This happened also during the lifetime of Mahavira and only two years after Jamali's schism. Tissagutta's followers were called Jivapar Siyas. They controverted Mahavira's view that the soul is permeated in all the atoms of the body.

The third schism was led by Asadha at Seyaviya, 214 years after the death of Mahavira. Asadha's followers were called Avattiyas, and they held that there was no difference between Gods, saints, kings and other beings.

The fourth schism was started by Assamitta in Mihila 220 years after Mahavira's death. Assamita was a disciple of Kidinna who was a disciple of Mahagiri. Assamitta's followers were called Samuchchaya and they held that after the end of all life will come one day, the effects of good or bad deeds are immaterial.

The fifth schism was started by Ganga at Kullakatiriya, 228 years after the death of Mahavira. Ganga was a disciple of Dhanya Gutta, another disciple of Mahagiri. His followers were called Dokiriyas, and they held that two opposite feelings such as cold and warmth could be experienced at the same time.

The sixth schism arose in Antaranjiya and was started by Sadulaya, otherwise known as Rohagutta, 544 years 1 after the death of Mahavira. Sadulaya is said to have been the author of the Vaisheshika Sutras. His followers were called Terasiyas and they held that between life (Jiva) and non-life (Aliv), there is a third state 'no-Jiva'. According to the Kalpa-Sutra, the Terasiya sect was founded by Rohagutta a disciple of Mahagiri. 2 The seventh schism was led by Gotta Mahila at Dashapura, 584 years after Mahavira's death. His followers were called Abaddhiyas and they asserted that Jiva was not bounded by karma. No trace of these seven schisms is now left in the Jain religion.

The difference between the Svetambaras and the Digambaras

The total number of points by which the Digambaras differ from the Svetambaras is eighteen. These are listed below: The Digambaras do not accept the following Shvetambara beliefs:

1. A kevali needs food;

2. A kevali needs to evacuate (nihari);

3. Women can get salvation. (To get salvation a woman has according to the Digambaras to be born

again as a man).

4. The Shudras can get salvation;

5. A person can get salvation without forsaking clothes;

6. A householder can get salvation;

7. The worship of images having clothes and ornaments is permitted;

8. The monks are allowed to possess fourteen (specified) things;

9. The Tirthankara Mali was a woman;

10. The eleven of the original Angas (Canonical works) still exist;

11. Bharat Chakravarti attained kevali hood while living in his palace;

12. A monk may accept food from a Shudra;

13. Mahavira's embryo was transferred from one womb to another, and Mahavira's mother had fourteen auspicious dreams before he was born. The Digambaras believe that she had 16 such dreams;

14. Mahavira had a sickness due to the tejolesya of Goshala.

15. Mahavira had married and had a daughter.

16. A cloth offered by the Gods (devadiya) fell on the shoulders of a Tirthankara.

17. Marudevi went for her salvation riding an elephant;

18. A monk may accept alms from many houses

Seventeen

HISTORY OF DIGAMBARA

The history of the Digambaras after Mahavira can generally be divided into four periods. These periods differ from one another not because each of them necessarily had any special characteristic, but mainly because each of the preceding periods from the past is shrouded in more and more obscurity, with the result that we know practically nothing substantial about the first of these four periods, know a little more about the second, and so on.

These periods are as follows:

a)The first five or six centuries after Mahavira. i.e. the period between Mahavira and the beginning of the Christian era.

b) The eight centuries from the beginning of the Christian era. This may be called the period of the

Acharyas.

c) The period of the dominance of Bhattarakas, i.e. up to the 17th/18th century.

d) The period of reformation - 17th/18th century to the present day.

The First Six centuries As stated above, the first five or six centuries in the history of the Digambara sect are hidden in obscurity. We know almost nothing about the history of this sect as a separate Jain Church in these centuries.

(The reason most probably was that the two Churches had not till then separated, and as such, they had no separate history.)

The Digambaras, unlike the Svetambaras, have not written any history of their sect, and all that we have are some lists of successive patriarchs. Not much reliance can be placed on these lists for they were compiled many centuries later. The first list that we possess is the one inscribed in Shravanabelagola in about AD 600, which is almost eleven centuries after Mahavira. This Shravanabelagola succession list is as follows:

Mahavira Gautama-Lokacharya-Jambu- Vishnu Deva- Aparajita- Govardhana-Bhadrabahu Vishakha-Prostila - Karttikeya (Kshattrikarya)-Jaya- Nama (Naga)- SiddharthaDhritisena- Buddhila, etc.

It will be noticed that the difference with the Shvetambara list starts almost from the very beginning.

The name of Gautama as the successor of Mahavira is not mentioned in the Shvetambara list as given in the Kalpa-Sutra. The Kalpa Sutra explicitly mentions that only two Ganadharas, Indrabhuti and Sudharma, survived Mahavira, and it was Sudharma who succeeded Mahavira as head of the Church and no other Ganadhara left any spiritual descendants. Indrabhuti who was a Gautama by gotra is the person mentioned in the Digambara list as the first successor of Mahavira.

Both the sects are in agreement in asserting that Indrabhuti Gautama was a kevalin, but the Svetambaras deny that he ever headed the Church, or left any disciples. The confusion is carried on to the next name also. Many Digambara lists including the Shravanabelagola inscription say that Gautama's successor as the head of the Church was Lokacharya. The name Lohacharya is not known to the Svetambaras. Other Digambara lists (e.g. the one in the Harivamsa Purana) mention Sudharma as the successor of Gautama. Fortunately, Lohachara and Sudharma are the names of the same person. This is explicitly stated in Jambudvipa Pannati. In the Digambara list, Lok Acharya's and the Shvetambara list Sudharma's successor is Jambusavari. Here for the first and last time, the Digambara and Svetambara lists agree concerning the order of succession. (Digambaras and Svetambaras both agree that after Mahavira, only three persons, namely, Gautama, Sudharma, and Jambu became kevalins.) The next three names in the Shravanabelagola list (AD 600) are Vishnu Deva, Aparajita and Govardhana.

Later Digambara works such as the Harivamsa Purana (late 8th century) include the name of Nandimithra between Vishnudeva and Aparajita.

The present-day Digambaras accept this later list of four names. However, none of these names are known to the Svetambaras. They have instead of the following three names: Prabhava, Shayyambna (or Shayyambhava) and Yashodhara. Shayyambhava, as we have seen, was the author of the Dashavaikalika, one of the most important texts of the Svetambaras, but the Digambaras neither know his name nor recognize the book. The successor of Govard-hana in the Digambara list is Bhadrabahu. In the Shvetambara list, the corresponding place is occu-pied by two persons: Bhadrabahu and Sambhuta Vijaya who were joint patriarchs of the Church. Bhadrabahu is an important name for the Digam-baras. It was Bhadrabahu who had according to the Shravanabelagola inscription (AD 600) had predicted a famine in Ujjain which led the Jain community there to leave for South India under the leadership of one Prabha Chandra (or, according to the later versions, he led the Jain community (of

Magadh?) to South India). The difficulty can be solved if we accept that it was another Bhadrabahu who had taken the community there. This second Bhadrabahu appears as the 27th acharya in the Digambara list (the Svetambaras do not know him) and was an Upangi i.e. knower of one Anga only, and not a Shruta Kevali like Bhadrabahu I, who knew all the 12 Angas. Bhadrabahu II died 515 years after the Nirvana (i.e. in 12 BC) and we know that he belonged to South India, for the great Kundakunda who undoubtedly belonged to South India calls himself the pupil of Bhadrabahu. 1 The matter is slightly confusing here for according to the pattavalis of the Digambaras, Kundakunda was not the first but the fourth acharya after Bhandabahu II.

Eighteen

HISTORY OF SVETAMBARAS

The Svetambaras, as a distinctly separate, developed only after the Valabhi Council. This Council was held in the year 980 (or 993) after the death of Mahavira (about the middle of the 5th century AD) to collect the sacred texts and for reducing them to writing. It was presided over by Devardi Kshamasramna.

An important work of this period was the completion of the Kalpa Sutra of Bhadrabahu. The whole of the Kalpa Sutra cannot be ascribed to Bhadrabahu who had died 170 years after Mahavira. The Kalpa Sutra has three sections. The first section contains the Jinacaritra, "the biographies of the Jinas." The main portion of this section is the biography of Mahavira.

The second section of the Kalpa Sutra consists of the Ther avail, i.e. the list of the pontiffs, and also the name of the schools (Gana), their branches (Sakha) and names of the heads of the school. This list contains the names of the heads of the school. This list contains names of the pontiffs up to Devardi nearly 30 generations after Bhadrabahu.

Thus this list could not have been compiled by Bhadrabahu himself. The third section of the Kalpa Sutra contains the Samacari, or Rules for the ascetics, namely, the rules for the rainy season (Pajjusan). It has been conjectured that this, the oldest section of the Kalpa Sutra was the work of Bhadrabahu. Indeed the complete title of the Kalpa Sutra is Pajjosanakappa, though this name fits only the third section. The other two sections according to the tradition, were added later by Devarddhi. So far as an ordinary Shvetambara layman is concerned the Kalpa Sutra is his most important sacred text. It is revered almost in the same manner by him as the Bhagavad Gita is revered by an ordinary Hindu. The Kalpa Sutra in the present form is also the first text of the Shvetambara Church, not accepted by the Digambaras.

With the earlier literature of the Jains, i.e. the sayings of Mahavira and the principal Ganadharas, the Valabhi Council reduced to writing whatever the Council thought had been authentically handed down. These are the canonical books of the Sve-tambaras. They are called the Angas Upangas, etc. and number 45 in all.

The Digambaras do not accept them as authentic and canonical but do not reject them completely either. During the nearly 10 centuries that passed between the death of Mahavira and the Vallabhi Council, many scholars had written commentaries on these Angas, Upangas, etc. These commentaries are called Nijutis or Niryuktis.

All these commentaries would necessarily be considered Shvetambara literature. Similar would be the position of all the other Jain literature consid-ered not acceptable by the Digambaras. One such example would be the commentary by Umasvati or Umasvami on his own Tatvar Hadigama-Sutra. While the text of this work is acceptable to both the sects, the commentary by the author himself is rejected by the Digambaras. Yet another method of identifying a Shvetambara work is by the name itself. This method applies to mythologies only. While the Svetambaras call the mythologies to carry or Caritas the Digambara term for mythology is Purana, Thus the Ram epic Pauma-cariya by Vimala Suri may be called a Shvetambara work. This was composed 530 years after Mahavira's death, that is, in or about AD. (However, except for occasional differences, the tales described in both sets of the epics are essentially the same. In other words, but for the name, it would be difficult to assign the epics to anyone sect).

The Shvetambara monks composed a large number of commentaries between the 6th and 9th centuries. These later commentaries were called churnis. One churni on the Nandi- Sutra called Mandichurni mentions that a council had been held in Mathura also. This churni was completed in Saka 598, that is, 676 AD, i.e., after the Vallabhi Council.

The Mathura Council was presided over by Skandia. His name does not occur in the list of sthaviras of the Kalpa Sutra, but Jacobi notes in his translation of the Kalpa Sutra, that he might be the same as Sandilya mentioned 33rd in the list of the sthaviras. It is not clear what the results of this Mathura Council were. Probably the Council did not come to any final decision. Another important churni of this century is that of the Avashyak-Sutra by Jinadasagani.

This gives a long description of Mahavira's journeys during the 12 1/2 years that he wandered as an ascetic before attaining the kevala jnana. Jinadasagani must have obtained his facts from an earlier and reliable source, for his description of Mahavira's travels is considered more or less authentic. One important thing that happened during the fifth and sixth centuries, that is, during the Gupta period of Indian history was that the Jain iconography was standardized. This iconography is more or less the same for both Digambaras and Svetambaras, except of course for the fact that the Digambara images of the Tirthankaras do not have any clothes or ornaments. Two postures were standardized for these images: one standing, called the Kayotasaras, and the other sitting in the yogasana pose. The Tirthankaras in northern India all had the srivatsa mark on their chests.

They were also given distinguishing signs called Lanchanas and besides, each Tirthankara was given a pair of attendants, called yaksha and yakshini whose images are carved on the two sides of the Tirthankara. At the time of Mahavira, the Yakshas as we have seen, were popular local divinities and there were yaksha temples in all the towns of Magadh.

As the worship of Yakshas diminished, they became in the case of the Jains the attendants of the Tirthankaras. They, however, served a very useful purpose in Jain worship.

A Tirthankara does not answer the prayer of a devotee, and therefore no worshipper when he performs a puja in a temple asks for any gift from him. But if an uninstructed Shvetambara does ask a gift, his prayer would be answered not by the Tirthankara (who does not even hear it), but by the yaksha in attendance of the Tirthankara. A class of deities that became quite prominent during this period was the Vidyadevis. In the beginning, there was perhaps only one Vidyadevi, viz., Sarasvati, the Goddess of Learning. A Sarasvati image has been found even in the Kankali-tila remains in Mathura. This can be dated the latest to the end of the 3rd century (the year inscribed on the image is 54). Later, a new set of Vidya Devis was added to the Jain pantheon, and ultimately we have sixteen of them. Their names are Rohini, Prajnapti, Vajrashrinkhala, Vajrankusha, Apraticakra, Purushadatta, Kali, Mahakali, Gauri, Gandhari, SarvastraMahajvala, Manavi, Vairotya, Achchhupta, Manasi and Mahamanasi. All these sixteen can be seen depicted, for instance, in the famous Dilwara temple at Abu. None of these sixteen Vidya Devis carried the usual attributes of the Goddess of learning, viz. A book and a vina (lute). Also from their names, it appears that they were similar to the Buddhist 5 and Hindu Tantric Goddesses. It will also be noticed that the period when the Jain Vidya Devis evolved was the period of the heyday of the Tantrik movement in India.

FACTS ABOUT JAINISM

- Every living being has a soul.
- Every soul is potentially divine, with innate qualities of infinite knowledge, perception, power, and bliss.
- Jainists think of every living being like themselves, harming no one and be kind to all living beings.
- Every soul is born as a celestial, human, subhuman or hellish being according to its karmas.
- Every soul is the architect of its own life, here or hereafter.
- When a soul is free from karma, it becomes free and attains divine consciousness, experiencing infinite knowledge, perception, power, and bliss.
- Navakar Mantra is the fundamental prayer in Jainism and can be recited at any time of the

day.

- Non-violence includes compassion and forgiveness in thoughts, words, and actions toward all living beings and respecting the views of others.
- Jainism stresses the importance of controlling the senses including the mind, as they can drag one far away from the true nature of the soul.
- Limit possessions and lead a pure life that is useful to yourself and others. Owning an object by itself is not possessiveness; however, attachment to an object is. Non-possessiveness is the balancing of needs and desires while staying detached from our possessions.
- Enjoy the company of the holy and better qualified, be merciful to those afflicted souls and tolerate the perversely inclined.
- It is important not to waste human life in evil ways. Rather, strive to rise on the ladder of spiritual evolution.
- The goal of Jainism is the liberation of the soul from the negative effects of unenlightened thoughts, speech, and action.
- Jains mainly worship idols of Jinas, Arihant's and Tirthankars, who have conquered the inner passions and attained divine consciousness.
- Right View, Right Knowledge and Right Conduct (triple gems of Jainism) provide the way. There is no supreme divine creator, owner,

preserver or destroyer. The universe is self-regulated and every soul has the potential to achieve divine consciousness (Siddha) through its efforts. According to Jain philosophy, a soul in its pure form is God.

EPILOGUE

The Jains Today Of the two sects of the Jains the Sve-tambaras, as we have seen, belong mainly to western India, that is, to Gujarat and Rajasthan. They have spread from there for purposes of business to the rest of the country. The Digambaras, on the other hand, can be divided into two distinct geographical groups. The indigenous Jains of South India are all Digambaras. Professionally they are artisans and farmers and not ordinarily businessmen. They are tightly knit communities and their religious and social lives are controlled by the Bhattarakas. They do not have any kind of social intercourse with the North Indian Digambaras who in their turn are hardly aware of their existence except perhaps when they see them during pilgrimages to South India. Educationally also the South Indian Digambaras are not very advanced. Most of the Jains who write about their religious community thus ignore them.

They are remembered only when the past glories of Jainism in South India are considered. The Digambaras of North India are spread throughout eastern Rajasthan, Haryana, U.P., and Bihar, in small scattered communities.

Talking of Jains, it appears that the one great fear that pervades throughout the community is that of being lost in the great ocean that is Hinduism. This fear appears to be a recent one, and in any case perhaps not more than 50 years old. Formerly, (and even today among the rich) it was quite common for Shvetambara Jain Agravales and non- Jain Agrawales to intermarry, the bride adopting the religion of the husband. Indeed, the term Hindu was never used, the term for the religion of the non-Jain Agrawales being Vaishnava. Among the Osavales of Rajasthan today some are Jains and the others call themselves Vaishnavas. Things are, however, changing. Inter-marriages between the Jains and the non-Jains are not very much liked by the leaders of the Jain society today. "Now there is a growing tendency to eradicate every non-Jain element from the Jain community. As a result, many Jains have stopped keeping marital relations with the Hindus."

There is one interesting difference between Hinduism and Jainism. The Hindus
have no religious creed, but they have a large

literature on social customs and civil law.

These are known as the Dharmashastras. The Jains on the other hand, one might say, have a religious code of conduct enshrined in their five vows; but they do not have any ancient law book. Thus, for instance, marriage among the Hindus is a religious matter, while for the Jains it is more or less a contract. "It is not ordained in Jain religion to marry for the emancipation of the soul. Marriage is not concerned with life here-after! When no offerings are to be made to the forefathers, the question of discharging obligations due to departed ancestors does not arise. Jain scriptures do not lay down elaborate rules and regulations regarding marriage." The later day Jain religious books like the Adi Purana or the Trivarnikachara generally quote the corresponding Hindu rules for social matter. For instance, such books mention the same eight forms of marriages as are mentioned in the Manusmriti. In theory, the Jains also allow the remarriage of widows and quote the same shloka that occurs in the Hindu Parashara-Smriti based on which Ishvara Chandra Vidyasagar was able to get the law on the remarriage of the Hindu widows enacted. According to Nathuram Premi, the Jain work Dharma Pariksha (11th century) supports the view that the word patau occurring in this shloka means a legally married husband, even though the grammatically correct form for such meaning should be patyau. In any case widows' remarriage among the Jains follow the regional caste customs. It is not uncommon in the South, while it not socially favored in the North. In the matter of exogamy, the Jains follow the same rules as their Hindu neighbors. For instance, in the Karnataka region marriages between cross-cousins and even marriages between maternal uncles and nieces are quite common, while in the North the Jains leave out the same number of gotras as their Hindu neighbors do; and also observe the same rituals. Thus the marriage ceremony is considered to have been completed as soon as the saptapadi or a similar ritual, has been performed. There is a big difference between the Hindus and the Jains in their manner of treating the ascetics. Among the Hindus, an ascetic is for all practical purposes out-side the society. There is, in theory, no relationship between him and the lay society, unless of course, he becomes a God-man.

This is not the position among the Jains. The Jain ascetic maintains a life-long relationship with the lay society and is generally treated as a religious teacher. The society not only provides food and, if necessary, shelter to him but also maintains a constant watch on his behavior. No transgression of the ascetic vow is tolerated. For instance, one Jinavardhana who had become the 55th leader of the Shvetambara Kharataragachchha was removed from the Suri ship for breaking the fourth vow. Thus, since a Jain sadhu needs neither worry about his food nor is allowed to be away from the watch-full eyes of the society, so the only thing he can do to spend his time is to read and write. All through the ages, therefore, there have been innumerable writers among the Jain sadhus and the volume of writings they have produced is enormous. The quality, however, has not, except in rare cases, been commensurate with the quantity.

The Jain religious philosophy being practically frozen from the time of Mahavira, there is a little scope of speculation. The later philosophical books written by the Jain monks are, therefore, dry. The Jain monks have also composed many works based on the Jain mythology, but since they had to avoid everything even remotely connected with sensual love, there is little of poetic value in these writings. Nearly the whole of the vernacular literature of the medieval period of India is devotional. Here also, the Jains were at a disadvantage, for the Jain religion has no place for devotional fervor. Even though their writings may not have any lasting value as literature, the studious life that the Jain ascetics had to lead meant that they had to be provided with libraries. Thus book collections, "Grantha Bhandaras", exist at every place where there is a group of Jain families living. Dr. K. C. Kasliwal has enumerated 100 such collections in Rajasthan alone, in his work the Jain Granth Bhandar in Rajasthan.

These collections contain not only Jain religious works but many secular books such as the works of Kalidas and sometimes works on music also. One valuable contribution of the Jains to Indian culture is the innumerable beautiful temples that they have built all over the country. Some of them being in out of the way places have escaped the hands of the idol-breakers. But due to this very fact, some of them are not well known even today. As examples, one might mention the temples at Ranakpur in the Pali district in Rajasthan, and the 31 Jain temples at Deogarh (Lalitpur Tehsil in Jhansi district). This latter place has more than a thousand Jina images. One of them has been described as "one of the greatest masterpieces ever created on Indian soil". The Jain merchants since ancient times have been well- known for their wealth. Not everybody was rich, but a remarkable thing is that some of the families who were the richest in a city and were thus given the title of Nagara- Seth by the Mughals, remain rich even now. Two examples are, Seth Kasturbhai Lalbhai the Nagara-Seth of Ahmedabad, and Jivaraj Walchand Gandhi, the

Nagara-Seth of Sholapur.6 Many Jains have utilized their wealth well. In building charitable hospitals, schools, colleges, Dharamshala, and other such institutions the contribution of the Jains has been proportionately many times higher than that of the rest of the population of the country.

REFERENCES

1 Sacred Books of the East Vol. XXII, p. xxii fn. gives the reference to Weber, Ind. Stud. XVI, p.469

2 The Uttaradhayana Sutra XXIII mentions Keshi as a disciple of Parshvanatha. This is one of the several indications that Parshvanatha was a historical person.

3. Uttaradhayana Sutra XXIII, 87, in Sacred Books of the East, Vol.XLV, p. 128

4. A.A.Macdonell, India's Past, pp. 70-71

5. Rigveda, IX, 113. 9-11

6. Rigveda, IX, 104.2.

7. A late hymn in the Rigveda (X, 136) mentions the existence of munis. The meaning of the hymn is not clear. Perhaps a Muni was a person with supernatural power.

8. Sacred Books of the East, Vol. XV, p. 163

9. The Brihadarnyka Upanishad (II.I.I) also mentions an Ajatashatru, contemporary with Janak but

167

he belonged to Kashi, not Magadh.

10. Kosala and Videh do not appear in the early Vedic literature. They are first mentioned in the Satapatha Brahman (I.4.1.10ff) which relates the story of the spread of the Aryan (Vedic?) culture. Vedic Age p. 258

11. Vedic Index, Vol. II, p.342

12. Ibid., p.343

13. Goetz in Encyclopedia of World Art, VIII, p. 792.

14. Studies in the Origin of Buddhism, p.317

15. The Wonder that was India, p. 246

16. R. N. Dandekar, Some Aspects of the History of Hinduism, p.28

17. Ibid., pp.1-2

18. Samanna-Phala Sutra in sacred Books of the Buddhist, Vol. II, p.77.

19. These incidents are given in Jinadasa's Churni, a 7th century commentary on the Avashayaka Sutta. Thought a late work, the description appears to be reliable.

20. The sacred Books of the Buddhist. Vol. II, pp.108-136

21. Sacred Books of the East, Vol. xiv, p.417

22. Jacobi in the Sacred Books of the East Vol. XLV, xxix

23. Jacobi in the Sacred Books of the East Vol. XLV, pp. xxvii- xxxiii

24. History of Philosophy, Eastern and Western. VolI., p.133

25. Mahabharat, Shanty P. ch.38

26. This point has been examined in greater detail in chapter VII.

27. Rys Davids, the translators of the above passage has suggested that the series of riddles in this difficult passage were probably intended to be ironical imitation of the Niganthas's way of talking. (Sacred books of the Buddhists Vol. II, p.75 fn).

28. Macdonell and Keith, Vedic Index, Vol. II, p. 182

29. For instance, in the Acaranga Sutra in Sacred Books of the East Vol. XXII, p.28. In Jain Prakrit the word is written as Niggantha and in Pali , as Nigantha. In Sanskrit form is Nirgrantha.

30. Sacred Books of the East, : Vol. XLV, pp. 419-35

31. Ibid., Vol. XLV, pp. xxx-xxxi

32. Ibid., Vol. XLV, pp. 419-35 33. Ibid., pp. xxx-xxxii

33. Schurbing, The Doctrine of Jains p. 23.

34. The Digambaras call these lives Purana whereas Svetambaras call them Charitras.

35. Schubring op. cit. p.20

36. Winternitz, A History of India Literature Vol. II, p.495

37. A reference to the Chakravartins possessing

14 is found in the Hindu Vishnu Purana also. Of these 14 Jewels, 7 are inanimate, viz. Cakra (wheel), rath (chariot), khanga (sword), charm (shield), dhvaja (flag), nidhi (treasury), and 7 are animate, viz. wife, priest, commander of the army, charioteers foot soldiers, troops mounted on horses, and troops mounted on elephants. Other books give other lists.

38. Bk.2. ch.1

39. The term "Aristameni", which occurs sometimes in the Vedic literature, for instance, in Rigveda X. 178.1, is not the name of any person

40. The fact that Trishala, the mother of Mahavira, was a sister of king Chetaka is not mentioned in the canon. We learn about this only from Avashayakachurni of Jinadasagani (7th century AD)

41. Sacred Books of the East Vol. XXII. p. xv

42. Winternitz, op. cit. 443

43. Acaranga Sutra in Sacred Books of the East Vol. XXII, p. 194

44. Sacred Books of the East Vol. XXII. p.84

45. Sacred Books of the East Vol. XXII, p.411

46. The account of Mahavira's travel as given in the Avashakchurni has been summarized above from J. C. Jain Life in Ancient India, pp. 257-261

47. Schubrihg, op. cit. P. 44

48. There is some similarity here with the life of the Buddha. The Lalitvistara describes the life of the Buddha in some detail to the time he attained

Buddhahood and traveled to Sarnath to preach his first sermon. This was when he was 36. For the remaining 44 years of the Buddha's life we have little connected details.

49. Helen M. Johnson has translated this work by Hemachandra in six volumes. The Oriental Institute, Baroda, published the translation. Vol. VI, which is used here extensively, was published in 1962.

50. That Jamali was Priyadarshna's husband, is not mentioned in the canon though his name occurs several times in the canonical texts. The later commentaries however say that Jamali was the husband of Priyadarshana, daughter of Mahavira.

51. H. Jacobi mentions in his article on Jainism in the Encyclopedia of Religion and Ethics, Vol. VII, that 527 BC was the date given by Shvetambera of Mahavira's Nirvana, while Digambers place the event 18 years later. This does not seem to be correct. Trilokasara (shloka 850), a Digambra's work mentions that Mahavira's Nirvana took place 605 years and 5 months before the shaka king (AD 78). This gives 527 BC as the date of Mahavira's Nirvana. Another Digambera work Tiloypannati gives three dates dates for Mahavira's Nirvana . Two of them absurdly give old dates, but the third one (sl. 1499) agrees with Trilokasara.

52. Sacred Books of the East Vol. XXII, p.205

14. Sutrakritanga in Sacred Books of the East, Vol. XLV, p.409

53.H. Jacobi in his Introduction to Hemachandra's Parishishtaparyam, p. xiv.

54. The figures in the brackets refer to the canto and shloka numbers in the Asiatic Society edition of Hemchandra's sthaviravali. The portions within inverted commas are Jacobi's summaries of these shlokas.

55. The Buddhist version of how Kunala was blinded is different. It is said that Tishyaraksha, the chief queen of Ashoka, fell in love with Kunala who tried to desist his stepmother. In her fury she caused him to be blind; or Kurala tore out his own eyes to prove his innocence. Cambridge History of India, Vol. I. P. 451)

56. Ashoka's successor, according to some Buddhist sources, was Konala whose successor, according to some Buddhist sources, was Kunala whose successor was his son Samprati. Cambridge History of India, Vol. I, p. 461

57. "Evidently Sthulabhadra's eldest sister is meant."(Note by Jacobi)

58. Appendix V.

59. Introduction to the Sthaviravali, p. xvii

60. "Rohagutta was a disciple of Suhasti." (Jacobi's note). This does not appear to be correct. According to the Kalpa Sutra Rohagutta was a disciple of

Mahagiri, colleague of Suhastin. This makes the matter more confusing.

61.Jacobi himself questions the dates of the various schisms given in the Avashyak Nirukti. The 4th schism was started by Assamita, who was a disciple of Kodinna, a disciple of Mahagiri, in 220 AV. and the 5th schism was started by Ganga who was the disciple of Dhanagutta, disciple of Mahagiri in 228 AV. Thus the difference between the periods of the two heresies both started by prashishyas of Mahagiri is eight years. But the 6th schism that was since we know that Mahagiri and Suhastin were contemporaries, the difference between the ages of their prashisyas could not be as much as 300 years

62. Sacred Books of the East, Vol. XXII, p. 288.

63. Select Inscriptions, p. 360.

64. Pravasi (Bengali), Vaishakha B. S 1327 (AD 1934), pp. 63, 72.

65. At Pakbira in the Manbhum district, a colossal naked figure of Vira under the name of Bhiram is still worshipped by the people. (Distt. Gasetteer of Manbhum, p. 51).

66. P.C. Roy Choudhary, Jainism in Bihar, Patna, 1956, P. 46. A photograph of the 2.25 meters high image has been reproduced in a plate facing P. 56 of this book. The caption there says that it is the image of Bahubali. This does not appear to be correct. Bahubali has creepers entwining his legs. There

are no creepers in this image. The lotus symbol on the pedestal shows that the image is either of the Tirthankara Padmaprabhanatha whose symbol is Red Lotus or of the Tirthankara Naminatha whose symbol is blue Lotus. So far as is known Bahubali is not worshipped in North India.

67. P.C. Roy Choudhary, Jainism in Bihar, Patna, 1956, p. 46. A Photograph of the 2.25 meters high image has been reproduced in a plate facing p. 56 of this book. The caption there says that it is the image of Bahubali. This does not appear to be correct. Bahubali has creepers entwining his legs. There are no creepers in this image. The Lotus symbol on the pedestal shows that the image is either of the Tirthankara Padmaprabhanatha whose symbol is Red Lotus or of the Tirthankara Naminatha whose symbol is Blue Lotus. So far as is known, Bahubali is not worshipped in North India.

68. Select Inscriptions, p. 213.

69. 'Arhant' is the term for saints both in Jainism and Buddhism. The reference here is clearly to the Jain saints, for the Jain formula of Namokkara or nokara is: Namo arihantam namo sidhanam Namo ayariyanam namo uvajhayanam Namo lo-e savva sahunam. The Buddhist formula of vandana in the Petakoppadesa is: Namo Sammasambuddhanam Paramthadassinam Shiladiguna-paramippattanam.

70. This line in the inscription has been read by Jayaswas as "Nandaraja-nitam ca kalingaJinam san-nivesa..., B.M. Barua, on the other hand reads here Nandaraja-jitan ca Kalingajanasan (n)i(ve)sam...... (Indian Historical Quarterly, Vol. XIV, p.468.) He translates the relevant passage as "...and compelled Brihaspatimitra, the king of the Magadh people, to bow down at his feet, (did something in connection with) the settlements of the Kalinga people subjugated by the king Nanda,...... carried the wealth......" Barua's reading would thus demolish the theory of the Kalinga-Jina' completely.

71. Barua thinks that Jayaswal's translation here of "relic depository" is wrong. Barua reads here, "the Arhat resting place," for fulfilling the rainy season vow.

72. Schubring, the Doctrine of the Jains, p. 48.

73. H. Goetz, in the Encyclopedia of World Art, Vol. VIII, p 788.

74. Debala Mitra, Udayagiri and Khandagiri, 1960, p. 6.

75. Ibid., pp. 6-7.

76. This date has been suggested on paleographic evidence.

77. Though the year Shaka 388 (AD 466-67) is clearly mentioned in this inscription, the writing is of the 8th or 9th century. From this it has been conjectured that it is a forged document. It is

likely, however, that it is the copy of a 5th century document. (A. K. Chatterjee, A Comprehensive History of Jainism, pp. 137- 38 and 324).

78. Jain Shilalekha Sangraha, Vol. I, pp. 1-2.

79. W. Schubring, op. cit., p 52.

80. M. Winternitz, A History of Indian literature, P. 476.

81. J. P. Singh, op. Cit., p. 101.

82. Ibid.

83. Ibid. p. 98.

84. K. A. Nilakanta Sastri & V. Ramsub Ramniam, "Aundy," in Mahavira and his Teachings, Bombay, 1977, p. 302.

85. I. Mahadevan, Corpus of the Tamil Brahmin Inscriptions, madras, 1966.

86. P. B. Desai, Jainism in South India, Sholapur, 1957, p. 24.

87.   Hemchandra mentions nothing about Dasharath, another grandson of Ashoka. That Dasharath was a historical person is proved from his three inscriptions bestowing on the Ajivika sect some caves in the Nagarjuni hills (Gaya district). Dasharath perhaps ruled over the eastern part of the Empire.

88. Different Puranas give different versions of the lists of kings. Thus Vishnu Purana says that after the reign of Andhra-Bhrityas, there would be seven Abhira and ten Gardhabhila kings who would

be followed by sixteen Shaka kings (Vishnu-Purana, Part IV, Ch. 24, SL. 51-52).

89. Winternitz, op. Cit., p. 589.

90. Papers on the Date of Kuniska, Leiden, 1968, pp. ix, 150-154. 30. This number in the bracket is the inscription number in the Jain-Shila-lekha Sangraha, Vol. II.

91. Hiven Tsang, when he passed through Mathura in the seventh century mentioned, that there were good numbers of Buddhist stupas in Mathura. "One of them built by the venerable Upagupta was on a hill, the sides of which have been excavated to allow the construction of cells. The approach is by a ravine." Hiuen Tsang's description has been doubted on the basis that there are no hills near about Mathura, Growse has suggested. "Upagupta's stupa may well have formed the raised center of the Kankali-tilla." (F. S. Growse, Mathura, a District Memoir, 2nd Ed. Allahabad, 1880, p. 110). Cunningham (1871) gave a description of the Kankali-tila 'hill' the higher portion of which at that time "had been repeatedly burrowed for bricks:" The "mound (was) 400 feet in length from west to east, and nearly 300 feet in breadth, with a mean height of 10 or 12 feet above the field. At the eastern end it (rose) to a height of 25 feet with a breadth of 60 feet at top, and about 150 feet at base. Kankali-tila contains without exception pure

Jain Monuments" Archaeological Survey of India, report 3, 1983, P. 19). It appears, therefore, that either Growse's conjecture that Kankali- tila was formally in Buddhist possession is wrong, and thus it was not this place which Hiuen-Tsang had visited; or if Growse is correct then the Jains had in later days i.e. after the visit of Hiuen Tsang removed all Buddhist remains from Kankali-tila.

92. Sircar, Select Inscriptions, pp. 156-157.

93. Not '42' as mentioned in the Jain Shila Lekha Sangraha, Vol. II, p. 12. See D. C. Sircar, Select Inscriptions, P. 120.

94. Negamesa or Harinegamesi was the God who under the orders of Shakra removed the embryo of Mahavira from the womb of Devandanda to that of Trishala: (Kalpa Sutra, in S. B. E., Vol. XXII, p. 229).

95. In Jain Shilalekha Saringraha, Vol. II, this profession is not mentioned. Luders, however, reads the word as "Ka (r) ppas (i) kasya", as the profession of the donor's husband. (Luders, Mathura Inscriptions, pp. 46- 47).

96. J. Prasad, Jain Sources of the History of India, p. 101.

97. Shrivatsa in the earlier images is generally a vertical line with an S- shaped mark on its left, and its mirror image on the right. Later the symbol changed into a lozenge shaped four-petalled flower. In Hinduism it represents "Shri" the Goddess of

fortune. It is the special mark of Vishnu. In Jainism Shrivatsa is found on the chests of Tirthankaras all over Northern India but not in South India. The symbol appears sometimes on the images of the Buddha also, but not on the chest. (C. Siva Ram Murti in Ancient India, No. 6, pp. 44-46).

98. See Appendix IV.

99. Corpus Inscriptionum Indicarum, Vol. III, No. 15.

100. For a discussion on the dates of these Schisms, see at the end of Chapter V.

101. Sacred Books of the East Vol. XXII, p.290.

102. Parishishtaparvam, Canto XI, SL. 1-4.

103. The Ajivikas, London, 1951.

104. Sacred Books of the East, Vol. XLV, p. 267n.

105. Sacred Books of the East, Vol. XLV, p. 245n.

106. Saletore, Medieval Jainism, p. 32.

107. Inscription No. 15 in Corpus Inscriptionum Indicarum, Vol. III.

108. Encylopedia Britannica, 15th Edn., Vol. 10, p.8.

109. Sacred Books of the East, Vol. XXII, p. 294n.

110. Jain Shila Lekha Sangraha, Vol. II, pp. 69-72.

111. Medieval Jainism, p. 32

About the Author

Lakshit Kankariya is an Instagram based motivational blogger and The host of the podcast Multipurpose with lakshit. The journey to write this book was not at all easy. It took him almost 14 months to analyze, read, speak, understand, and question about the religion so he can conclude this book and write something great so people get to know the truth. lakshit being Jain he was unknown to the truth of the religion and he says ' I am very happy that I got the chances and time to write this book for all the people who don't have the idea about it.

The reason to write this book is that he was doing is high school in France and being vegetarian and people questioning him for what is he is vegetarian. And explaining over and over to each person he met was not an easy thing. So he thought to write this book to give information to each one of them so they better understand the background of the religion and what it was meant to be.

You Can follow him :

Instagram: @lakshitkankariya

Facebook : @lakshitkankariya

Youtube : Lakshit Kankariya

And DM him on Instagram for wishing him good luck for his upcoming podcast.

Made in United States
North Haven, CT
17 July 2023

39167699R00117